Activity Book

EXPL🌐RING

FRENCH

Second Edition

Joan G. Sheeran

Consultants
Judy Gray Myrth
J. Patrick McCarthy

EMC Publishing, Saint Paul, Minnesota

ISBN 0-8219-1196-1

Published by EMC/Paradigm Publishing
875 Montreal Way
St. Paul, MN 55102

Printed in the United States of America
    4 5 6 7 8 9 10 XXX 99 98

Unit 1

 Give this girl a French name.

Give this boy a French name.

_____

_____

When the boy and girl meet for the first time, they introduce themselves. Write their names below and then complete their conversation.

(girl's name) _____ : Salut! Comment

t'_____ ?

(boy's name) _____ : _____ .

Et _____ ?

(girl's name) _____ : Je m'_____ .

(boy's name) _____ : E_____ .

B Match the French expression in column B with the situation in which you would use it in column A.

A

1. You accidentally bump into someone. _____

2. You ask a new classmate his or her name. _____

3. You wish your friend well at the beginning of the soccer game. _____

4. You wave as your friend walks away. _____

5. You say "good night" to your parents. _____

6. You greet a boy. _____

7. You greet a girl. _____

B

a) Salut, Étienne.

b) Au revoir.

c) Salut, Françoise.

d) Bonne nuit.

e) Pardon.

f) Bonne chance.

g) Comment t'appelles-tu?

C Complete these mini-dialogues with the appropriate words.

EXAMPLE: Janine: Bonjour, Monsieur Lebrun.

M. Lebrun: Bonjour, <u>Janine</u>.

1. Patrice: Salut, Marc.

   Marc: _____ , Patrice.

2. Robert: Comment t'appelles-tu?

   Marie: _____ m'appelle Marie.

3. Louis: Comment vas-tu?

   Jean: _____ , merci.

4. Charles: Annette, parles-tu allemand?

   Annette: _____ . Je parle allemand.

5. Yvette: Parles-tu italien?

   Guy: _____ . Je ne parle pas italien.

6. Nathalie: Merci, Anne.

   Anne: _____ , Nathalie.

7. Jean-Luc: Au revoir, Sylvie.

   Sylvie: Au revoir, Jean-Luc. À _____ .

D Write the French word for the principal language spoken in each country.

country   language

1. France   Je parle _____ .

2. Italie   Je parle _____ .

3. Espagne   Je parle _____ .

4. Allemagne   Je parle _____ .

5. Russie   Je parle _____ .

6. Angleterre   Je parle _____ .

E Can you guess how we say these other languages in English?

1. chinois   _____

2. arabe   _____

3. norvégien   _____

4. vietnamien   _____

5. japonais   _____

6. grec   _____

F Imagine that it's the first day of school. You and your partner play the roles of two students who haven't met yet. Carry on a short conversation in French in which each of you tries to find out as much information as you can about the other. Limit your questions to those you have already practiced in class and be sure to respond appropriately to your partner's questions or comments. For example, you might:

1) say "hello" or "hi" to your partner.
2) ask your partner what his or her name is.
3) ask your partner how he or she is.
4) ask your partner if he or she speaks German/Spanish/Italian/Russian.
5) tell your partner "good luck."
6) tell your partner "good-bye" and "see you later."

G Some French parents still follow the tradition of naming their child after the saint on whose feast day he or she was born. If the child is named after a saint whose feast day doesn't fall on his or her date of birth, the child can celebrate on each of these two days. For example, a girl named Christine who was born May 6 may celebrate on that date and again on July 24, her saint's day. Using the two lists of saints' names and days, answer the questions.

French • Name • Days

Janvier	Février	Mars	Avril	Mai	Juin
1 Jour de L'An	1 Ste. Ella	1 St. Aubin	1 St. Hugues	1 F. du Travail	1 St. Justin
2 St. Basile	2 Prés. Seigneur	2 St. Charles B.	2 Ste. Sandrine	2 St. Boris	2 Ste. Blandine
3 Ste. Geneviève	3 St. Blaise	3 St. Guénolé	3 St. Richard	3 Sts. Phil/Jacques	3 St. Kévin
4 St. Odilon	4 Ste. Véronique	4 St. Casimir	4 St. Isidore	4 St. Sylvain	4 Ste. Clotilde
5 St. Édouard	5 Ste. Agathe	5 Ste. Olive	5 Ste. Irène	5 Ste. Judith	5 St. Igor
6 St. Mélaine	6 St. Gaston	6 Mardi Gras	6 St. Marcellin	6 Ste. Prudence	6 St. Norbert
7 St. Raymond	7 Ste. Eugénie	7 Cendres	7 St. J.-B. de la S.	7 Ste. Gisèle	7 St. Gilbert
8 Épiphanie	8 Ste. Jacqueline	8 St. Jean de Dieu	8 Ste. Julie	8 Victoire 1945	8 St. Médard
9 Ste. Alix de Ch.	9 Ste. Apolline	9 Ste. Françoise	9 St. Gautier	9 St. Pacôme	9 Ste. Diane
10 St. Guillaume	10 St. Arnaud	10 St. Vivien	10 St. Fulbert	10 Ste. Solange	10 Pentecôte
11 St. Paulin	11 N.-D. Lourdes	11 Carême	11 St. Stanislas	11 Ste. Estelle	11 St. Barnabé
12 Ste. Tatiana	12 St. Félix	12 Ste. Justine	12 St. Jules	12 St. Achille	12 St. Guy
13 Ste. Yvette	13 Ste. Béatrice	13 St. Rodrigue	13 Ste. Ida	13 F. Jeanne d'Arc	13 St. Ant. de Pad.
14 Ste. Nina	14 St. Valentin	14 Ste. Mathilde	14 St. Maxime	14 St. Mathias	14 St. Élisée
15 St. Rémi	15 St. Claude	15 Ste. Louise Marill.	15 Rameaux	15 Ste. Denise	15 Ste. Germaine
16 St. Marcel	16 Ste. Julienne	16 Ste. Bénédicte	16 St. Benoît-J. L.	16 St. Honoré	16 St. J.-F. Régis
17 Ste. Roseline	17 St. Alexis	17 St. Patrice	17 St. Anicet	17 St. Pascal	17 Trin./F. d. Pères
18 Ste. Prisca	18 Ste. Bernadette	18 St. Cyrille	18 St. Parfait	18 St. Éric	18 St. Léonce
19 St. Marius	19 St. Gabin	19 St. Joseph	19 Ste. Emma	19 St. Yves	19 St. Romuald
20 St. Sébastien	20 Ste. Aimée	20 St. Hébert	20 Ste. Odette	20 St. Bernardin	20 St. Silvère
21 Ste. Agnès	21 St. Pierre Dam.	21 Ste. Clémence	21 St. Anselme	21 St. Constantin	21 St. Rodolphe
22 St. Vincent	22 Ste. Isabelle	22 Ste. Léa	22 Pâques	22 St. Émile	22 St. Alban
23 St. Barnard	23 St. Lazare	23 St. Victorien	23 St. Georges	23 St. Didier	23 Ste. Audrey
24 St. François Sal.	24 St. Modeste	24 Ste. Cath. Su.	24 St. Fidèle	24 St. Donatien	24 Fête-Dieu
25 Conv. st Paul	25 St. Roméo	25 Annonciation	25 St. Marc	25 Ste. Sophie	25 St. Prosper
26 Ste. Paule	26 St. Nestor	26 Ste. Larissa	26 Ste. Alida	26 St. Bérenger	26 St. Anthelme
27 Ste. Angèle	27 Ste. Honorine	27 St. Habib	27 Ste. Zita	27 Fête des Mères	27 St. Fernand
28 St. Thomas A.	28 St. Romain	28 St. Gontran	28 Ste. Valérie	28 St. Germain	28 Ste. Irénée
29 St. Gildas	29 St. Auguste	29 Mi-Carême	29 Souv. Déportés	29 St. Aymar	29 Sacré-Cœur
30 Ste. Martine		30 St. Amédée	30 St. Robert	30 St. Ferdinand	30 St. Martial
31 Ste. Marcelle		31 St. Benjamin		31 Ascension	
		Printemps : 20 Mars			Été : 21 Juin

1. Who is the saint whose feast day corresponds to your birthday?

   _____

2. Find the saint whose name most closely resembles yours. Who is this saint and when is his or her feast day?

   _____

3. Julie was born on February 8. Are her birthday and her saint's day identical?

   _____

French • Name • Days

Juillet	Août	Septembre	Octobre	Novembre	Décembre
1 St. Thierry	1 St. Alphonse	1 St. Gilles	1 Ste. Thér. E.-J.	1 Toussaint	1 Ste. Florence
2 St. Martinien	2 St. Julien	2 Ste. Ingrid	2 St. Léger	2 Défunts	2 Avent
3 St. Thomas	3 Ste. Lydie	3 St. Grégoire	3 St. Gérard	3 St. Hubert	3 St. Franç.-Xavier
4 St. Florent	4 St. J.-M. Viann.	4 Ste. Rosalie	4 St. Franç. d'Ass.	4 St. Charles Borr.	4 Ste. Barbara
5 St. Ant.-Mar.	5 St. Abel	5 Ste. Raïssa	5 Ste. Fleur	5 Ste. Sylvie	5 St. Gérald
6 Ste. Marietta G.	6 Transfiguration	6 St. Bertrand	6 St. Bruno	6 Ste. Bertille	6 St. Nicolas
7 St. Raoul	7 St. Gaétan	7 Ste. Reine	7 St. Serge	7 Ste. Carine	7 St. Ambroise
8 St. Thibaut	8 St. Dominique	8 Nat. V.-Marie	8 Ste. Pélagie	8 St. Geoffroy	8 Imm. Concept.
9 Ste. Amandine	9 St. Amour	9 St. Alain	9 St. Denis	9 St. Théodore	9 St. Pierre Fourier
10 St. Ulrich	10 St. Laurent	10 Ste. Inès	10 St. Ghislain	10 St. Léon	10 St. Romaric
11 St. Benoît	11 Ste. Claire	11 St. Adelphe	11 St. Firmin	11 Victoire 1918	11 St. Daniel
12 St. Olivier	12 Ste. Clarisse	12 St. Apollinaire	12 St. Wilfried	12 St. Christian	12 Ste. J.-F. Chant.
13 Sts. Henri/Joël	13 St. Hippolyte	13 St. Aimé	13 St. Géraud	13 St. Brice	13 Ste. Lucie
14 Fête Nationale	14 St. Evrard	14 Sainte Croix	14 St. Juste	14 St. Sidoine	14 Ste. Odile
15 St. Donald	15 Assomption	15 St. Roland	15 Ste. Térésa	15 St. Albert	15 Ste. Ninon
16 N.-D. Mt. Carm.	16 St. Armel	16 Ste. Édith	16 Ste. Edwige	16 Ste. Marguerite	16 Ste. Alice
17 Ste. Charlotte	17 St. Hyacinthe	17 St. Renaud	17 St. Baudouin	17 Ste. Élisabeth	17 St. Judicaël
18 St. Frédéric	18 Ste. Hélène	18 Ste. Nadège	18 St. Luc	18 Ste. Aude	18 St. Gatien
19 St. Arsène	19 St. Jean Eudes	19 Ste. Émilie	19 St. René	19 St. Tanguy	19 St. Urbain
20 Ste. Marina	20 St. Bernard	20 St. Davy	20 Ste. Adeline	20 St. Edmond	20 St. Théophile
21 St. Victor	21 St. Christophe	21 St. Mathieu	21 Ste. Céline	21 Prés. V.-Marie	21 St. Pierre Canis.
22 Ste. Marie-Mad.	22 St. Fabrice	22 St. Maurice	22 Ste. Salomé	22 Ste. Cécile	22 Ste. Franç.-Xav.
23 Ste. Brigitte	23 Ste. Rose	23 St. Constant	23 St. Jean de C.	23 St. Clément	23 St. Armand
24 Ste. Christine	24 St. Barthélemy	24 Ste. Thècle	24 St. Florentin	24 Ste. Flora	24 Ste. Adèle
25 St. Jacques M.	25 St. Louis	25 St. Hermann	25 St. Crépin	25 Christ-Roi	25 Noël
26 Ste. Anne	26 Ste. Natacha	26 Sts. Côme/Dam.	26 St. Dimitri	26 Ste. Delphine	26 St. Étienne
27 Ste. Nathalie	27 Ste. Monique	27 St. Vincent de P.	27 Ste. Émeline	27 St. Séverin	27 St. Jean Apôtre
28 St. Samson	28 St. Augustin	28 St. Venceslas	28 St. Simon	28 St. Jacqu. de M.	28 Sts. Innocents
29 Ste. Marthe	29 Ste. Sabine	29 St. Michel	29 St. Narcisse	29 St. Saturnin	29 St. David
30 Ste. Juliette	30 St. Fiacre	30 St. Jérôme	30 Ste. Bienvenue	30 St. André	30 Sainte Famille
31 St. Ignace	31 St. Aristide		31 St. Quentin		31 St. Sylvestre

Automne : 22 Septembre

Hiver : 21 Décembre

4. When would David celebrate his saint's day?

_____

5. What saint's name most closely resembles the name Michael? When is his saint's day?

_____

6. Whose feast day is February 14?

_____

7. What saint's name most closely resembles the name Ann? When would she celebrate her saint's day?

_____

8. Are there more male saints or female saints whose feast days fall in October?

_____

H Circle the following French words, expressions and names in the letter grid. The letters may go forward or backward; they may go up, down, across or diagonally.

1. tu parles français
2. allemand
3. russe
4. italien
5. à demain
6. espagnol
7. anglais
8. s'il te plaît
9. au revoir
10. pas mal

11. courtoisies
12. comment
13. enchanté
14. bien merci
15. Monique
16. Bertrand
17. salut
18. bonjour
19. à bientôt
20. oui

```
                    A  I  B  E  G  A  F  T  B
                    O  E  V  K  I  O  U  E  S  U  S
                    R  C  N  S  R  U  O  J  N  O  B  L  U
                 P  U  M  N  I  A  Q  H  U  P  R  A  D  A  O
              T  U  P  A  R  L  E  S  F  R  A  N  C  A  I  S  A
           I  J  I  S  H  B  T  L  N  B  M  O  D  M  D  K  G  T  V
        S  A  T  I  U  I  S  E  C  W  Q  R  N  E  O  E  U  T  N  O  P
     S  W  C  R  Q  E  T  A  P  I  A  J  A  L  L  E  M  A  N  D  A  I  E
  C  A  D  S  N  N  V  O  I  L  M  A  I  R  M  I  S  A  J  C  U  B  N  S  U
  M  O  I  T  M  L  D  T  B  A  G  P  F  H  N  L  R  I  I  R  M  C  U  P  R
  L  K  U  E  H  E  K  N  C  I  E  N  E  E  M  I  X  N  S  A  H  O  Y  A  B
  E  A  R  R  I  J  G  E  N  T  O  F  A  M  O  S  L  R  F  A  L  M  I  G  S
  L  C  L  A  T  U  O  I  V  D  I  G  R  V  N  K  T  E  N  B  A  M  E  N  O
  I  D  R  Z  A  O  E  B  C  F  O  A  E  Q  I  D  R  T  A  F  L  E  G  O  Z
  A  N  A  B  L  M  I  A  I  N  E  R  T  H  Q  A  E  I  H  A  X  N  E  L  J
  N  A  E  Q  I  I  P  S  O  Z  U  B  G  N  U  J  P  W  M  C  N  T  A  U  E
  I  R  E  Y  E  D  E  O  I  A  U  C  W  I  E  D  K  S  F  A  Y  A  I  I  L
  O  T  K  O  N  G  T  Y  C  E  T  V  E  X  G  E  A  F  O  L  E  D  H  J  A
  X  R  O  N  T  Z  F  R  U  S  S  E  F  I  L  P  F  A  B  G  O  L  C  S  H
  U  E  I                                            O        U  I
  S  B                                               M        E
```

Unit 2

A Answer each question in French.

1. What do you use to make sure a line is straight?

   _____

2. What do you write on paper with?

   _____

3. What do many people display outside their homes on the Fourth of July?

   _____

4. What does a teacher sit down on?

   _____

5. In what can you keep notes?

   _____

6. What do you use to sharpen a pencil?

   _____

B Name in French the classroom object most closely associated with the following cues.

1. 9:00, 5:30, 1:45, 7:52

   _____

2. Costa Rica, Belgium, Somalia, China

   _____

3. *The Adventures of Huckleberry Finn, Moby Dick, Sleeping Beauty*

   _____

4. still life, landscape, portrait, oil

   _____

5. ball point, felt tip, fountain

   _____

C Answer the question *Qu'est-ce que c'est?* by writing the French for the expression in parentheses.

1. C'est un _____ . (wall)

2. C'est une _____ . (classroom)

3. C'est une _____ . (board eraser)

4. C'est un _____ . (bookcase)

5. C'est une _____ . (map)

6. C'est une _____ . (window)

D How many items do you have in your backpack, book bag or pencil case for which you know the French word? List these items in French.

_____

_____

_____

_____

_____

_____

E Find your way through the classroom. As you trace your route from the entrance arrow labeled *Entrée* to the exit arrow labeled *Sortie*, list in French the classroom objects you encounter.

_____

_____

_____

_____

_____

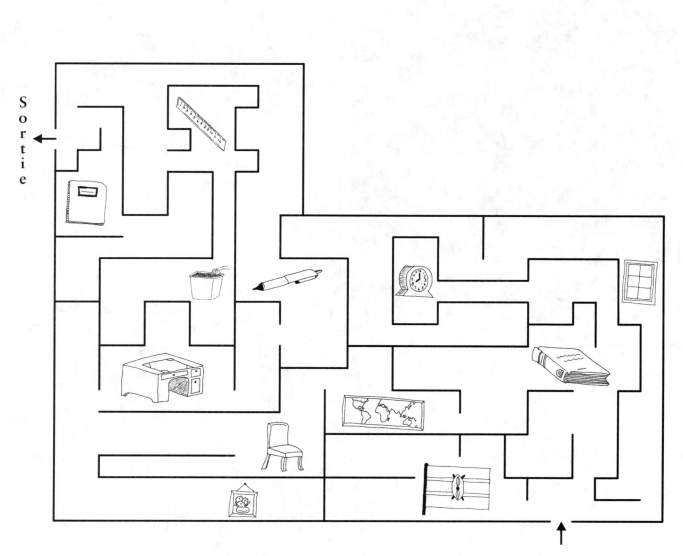

F Look at the advertisements for various objects you might find in a classroom and answer the following questions. A new word you will need to know is *cartable* (book bag).

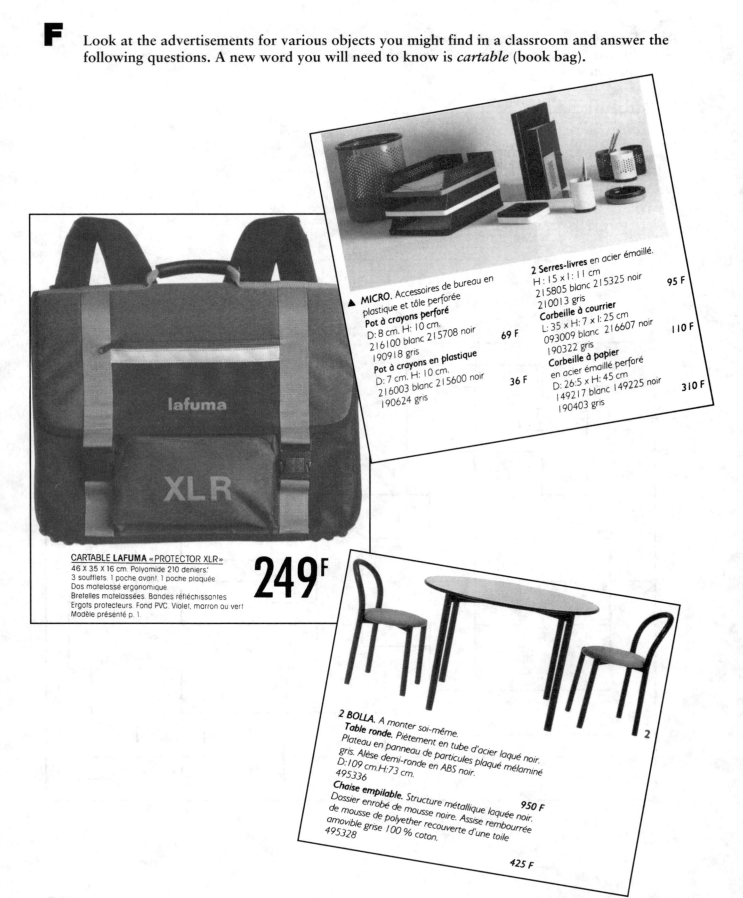

▲ **MICRO.** Accessoires de bureau en plastique et tôle perforée

Pot à crayons perforé
D: 8 cm. H: 10 cm.
216100 blanc 215708 noir
190918 gris
69 F

Pot à crayons en plastique
D: 7 cm. H: 10 cm.
216003 blanc 215600 noir
190624 gris
36 F

2 Serres-livres en acier émaillé.
H: 15 x l: 11 cm
215805 blanc 215325 noir
210013 gris
95 F

Corbeille à courrier
L: 35 x H: 7 x l: 25 cm
093009 blanc 216607 noir
190322 gris
110 F

Corbeille à papier
en acier émaillé perforé
D: 26:5 x H: 45 cm
149217 blanc 149225 noir
190403 gris
310 F

CARTABLE **LAFUMA** « PROTECTOR XLR »
46 X 35 X 16 cm. Polyamide 210 deniers:
3 soufflets. 1 poche avant. 1 poche plaquée
Dos matelassé ergonomique.
Bretelles matelassées. Bandes réfléchissantes
Ergots protecteurs. Fond PVC. Violet, marron ou vert
Modèle présenté p. 1.
249F

2 BOLLA. A monter soi-même.
Table ronde. Piètement en tube d'acier laqué noir.
Plateau en panneau de particules plaqué mélaminé
gris. Alèse demi-ronde en ABS noir.
D:109 cm. H:73 cm.
495336
950 F

Chaise empilable. Structure métallique laquée noir.
Dossier enrobé de mousse noire. Assise rembourrée
de mousse de polyether recouverte d'une toile
amovible grise 100 % coton.
495328
425 F

1. How many francs does the table cost?

   _____

2. If there are five francs to the dollar, how much does the table cost in dollars?

   _____

3. What is the shape of the table?

   _____

4. What fabric covers the chairs' seats?

   _____

5. How much does each chair cost in francs?

   _____

6. How much does the book bag cost in francs? What is one color it comes in?

   _____

   _____

7. Which pencil holder is more expensive, the plastic one or the perforated one? How much does it cost in francs?

   _____

   _____

8. How much do the bookends cost in francs?

   _____

9. How much does the wastepaper basket cost in francs?

   _____

G Unscramble the words.

1. teripune _____

2. itopen _____

3. mogem _____

4. latubae _____

5. rutpepi _____

6. elvir _____

7. legrooh _____

8. arbeuu _____

H Choose any ten classroom objects. As you point to each one, ask your partner what it is. Keep a record of how many objects your partner correctly identifies. Then reverse roles. This time you identify the objects your partner points out. See who can name the most items correctly.

EXAMPLE: You ask: Qu'est-ce que c'est?

Your partner answers: C'est un cahier.

Unit 3

A Select the word from the list that is most closely associated with the following commands.

eyes   hand   chair   mouth   feet   ears

1. Parle.   _____

2. Écoute.   _____

3. Assieds-toi.   _____

4. Écris.   _____

5. Va au tableau.   _____

6. Lis.   _____

B How would you tell your friend to do the following things in French? Circle the correct command.

1. Sit down.

   a) Parle.

   b) Assieds-toi.

2. Raise your hand.

   a) Va au tableau.

   b) Lève la main.

3. Close the book.

   a) Ferme le livre.

   b) Ouvre le livre.

4. Answer the question.

   a) Réponds à la question.

   b) Complète la question.

5. Say it in French.

   a) Dis-le en français.

   b) Écris en français.

6. Take out paper.

   a) Répète les phrases.

   b) Prends une feuille de papier.

C To help you learn the French expressions in this lesson, your teacher tells you what to do in class. Put these commands in logical order, beginning with "1" for the first command, "2" for the second command, etc.

_____ Répète les phrases.

_____ Assieds-toi.

_____ Ferme le livre.

_____ Va au pupitre.

_____ Ouvre le livre.

_____ Prends le livre, un cahier et un crayon.

_____ Écris les phrases.

D Complete the commands by writing the French for the word in parentheses.

1. _____ au tableau. (Go)

2. _____ à la question. (Answer)

3. _____ le livre. (Open)

4. _____ la fenêtre. (Close)

5. _____ les phrases. (Read)

6. _____-le en français. (Say)

E Write the command you would say to your friend in each of the following situations.

1. You want your friend to speak French.

_____

2. You want your friend to read the book.

_____

3. You want your friend to answer the question.

_____

4. You want your friend to take out a pen.

_____

5. You don't want your friend to stand up.

_____

6. You want your friend to stop reading.

_____

F Mots croisés

Vertical

1. Opposite of "ouvre."
2. When you have a question, you "...la main."
3. «Je...français.»
4. «Va...tableau.»
5. «Réponds à la....»
7. What you read.
9. A boy's name in French that resembles "Anthony" in English.
10. Not bad.
12. What you do with a pen.
14. «Qui ne dit mot,....»
15. «...parles anglais?» (*And you*)
17. "Un...de craie."
20. «...une feuille de papier.»
21. «Qu'est-ce que c'...?»
22. Opposite of "ferme."
23. «...au tableau.»

Horizontal

1. What you write on.
6. "...revoir."
8. "Les objets de la salle de...."
11. «...en français.» (*Say it*)
13. What you do if you want to hear something.
14. «...les phrases.»
16. What you do to a novel.
18. «C'...une chaise.»
19. Where a student sits in class.
24. What the teacher writes on using chalk.
25. At the end of your arm.
26. Be seated.
27. Sentence.

G With a classmate play *Jacques dit*, the French version of "Simon says." First give your partner a command. If you say *Jacques dit* before the command, your partner should perform the action ordered. If you do not say *Jacques dit*, however, your partner should ignore your command. Keep giving orders until your partner either performs incorrectly or makes a motion when you have not said *Jacques dit*. Then it's your partner's turn to give orders. Perform your partner's commands until you slip up. See who can respond correctly to the most orders.

H I. When you give a command in French to someone you don't know very well or to several people at once, the command word often ends in *-ez*. For each of the advertisements, copy the *-ez* command word or words you find in it beside its number.

Nom: _____ Date: _____

1. _____

2. _____

3. _____

4. _____

5. _____

II. **Now see if you can match the letter of the ad's meaning in English with its number.**

1. _____ a) Win movie tickets.

2. _____ b) Play and win 100 videocassettes.

3. _____ c) Join a book club and get two books for only ten francs.

4. _____ d) Have your newspaper sent to your vacation address.

5. _____ e) Don't buy a different car without checking with this finance company.

Unit 4

A Match each word in column B with its corresponding numeral in column A.

	A			B
1.	2	_____	a)	treize
2.	8	_____	b)	quarante
3.	13	_____	c)	vingt et un
4.	5	_____	d)	deux
5.	21	_____	e)	huit
6.	40	_____	f)	cinq

B How many items are pictured? Circle the correct number.

1.   vingt   trois   dix   un

2.   quinze   neuf   quatre   quatorze

3.   sept   deux   huit   cinq

4.   un   cent   onze   dix

5.    onze   dix-huit   treize   trois

C   **Answer each question with the correct number.**

1. How many planets are there?

   a) sept   b) neuf

2. How many toes does a person have?

   a) dix   b) huit

3. How many rings are there in the Olympic symbol?

   a) dix   b) cinq

4. How many states form the United States?

   a) quarante-huit   b) cinquante

5. How many weeks are there in one year?

   a) douze   b) cinquante-deux

6. How many letters are there in the English alphabet?

   a) vingt-six   b) vingt

7. How many days are in the month of November?

   a) trente et un   b) trente

8. How many items make up a baker's dozen?

   a) treize   b) douze

9. How many minutes are there in one hour?

   a) soixante   b) seize

10. How many sides does a stop sign have?

    a) quatre   b) huit

D **Add the missing number to complete each series.**

1. quarante, _____ , soixante

2. dix-huit, _____ , vingt

3. six, _____ , huit

4. cinq, _____ , quinze

5. soixante-dix, _____ , quatre-vingt-dix

6. huit cents, neuf cents, _____

E **Fill in the blank with the French word for the missing number.**

EXAMPLE: Dix et <u>quinze</u> font vingt-cinq.

1. Quarante-huit divisé par _____ font huit.

2. Dix multiplié par sept font _____ .

3. Cinquante-neuf moins _____ font trente-deux.

4. Quinze et _____ font quarante-cinq.

5. Douze multiplié par _____ font cent vingt.

6. Quatre-vingts moins vingt font _____ .

F Unscramble the words.

1. xid   _____

2. rtneet _____

3. limel _____

4. atosnexi _____

5. zoen   _____

6. tuhi   _____

7. qicn   _____

8. cnet   _____

9. givtn _____

10. siort _____

G With your classmates play *Dring*. This game is similar to the English game "Buzz." Pick a number lower than 10, for instance, 7. To begin, all students must stand up. Each student counts off in French, starting with *zéro*. When the number 7, a number containing 7 or a multiple of 7 comes up, the student whose turn it is must say *Dring* instead of the number. (For example, between 0 and 30 students should say *Dring* instead of 7, 14, 17, 21, 27 and 28.) A student who responds incorrectly must sit down. The count picks up after the next student in line corrects the error by saying *Dring* or the right number, depending on the type of mistake made. The winner of the game is the last person to remain standing.

H Examine this section of the Paris telephone directory. It shows a partial listing for the last name Fabre. Answer the questions that follow based on the information in the directory. You will need to know some new words: *télécopieur* (fax), *voiture* (car) and *r* (street, abbreviation for *rue*). The number following a street address indicates a certain district of Paris. For example, *16ᵉ* indicates the 16th district.

FABRE Adeline bat kepler
	1 Terrasse Parc 19ᵉ	(1)40 34 36 29
>>	Adrien 11 r Présentation 11ᵉ	(1)43 57 25 44
>>	Adrien 11 r Présentation 11ᵉ	(1)48 05 64 24
>>	Adrien 5 r Vicq d'Azir 10ᵉ	(1)42 41 51 27
>>	Agnès 308 r Lecourbe 15ᵉ	(1)45 54 76 57
>>	Agnès 60 r Rendez Vous 12ᵉ	(1)43 41 41 76
>>	Alain 91 r Championnet 18ᵉ	(1)42 62 15 64
>>	Alain 247 r Crimée 19ᵉ	(1)42 41 24 88
>>	Alain médecin orl	
	32 av Georges Mandel 16ᵉ	(1)45 53 42 77
>>	Alain bois Vincennes	
	esplanade St Louis 12ᵉ	(1)48 08 78 47
>>	Albert 69 bd Richard Lenoir 11ᵉ	(1)43 55 61 36
>>	Albert 4 r Roquépine 8ᵉ	(1)42 65 76 81
>>	Albert 4 r Roquépine 8ᵉ	
	Téléphone de voiture	(1)46 89 29 84
>>	Albert 17 pl St Pierre 18ᵉ	(1)42 64 29 04
>>	Alexia 31 r Linné 5ᵉ	(1)47 07 67 08
>>	Alice 89 r Roquette 11ᵉ	(1)43 79 74 09
>>	Alicia 9 av St Ouen 17ᵉ	(1)46 27 11 83
>>	Aline 10 villa Croix Nivert 15ᵉ	(1)47 83 74 73
>>	Aline 6 r Jules Simon 15ᵉ	(1)42 50 98 39
>>	André 2 pl Léon Blum 11ᵉ	(1)43 79 22 92
>>	André 2 pl Léon Blum 11ᵉ	(1)43 79 52 64
>>	André avocat 44 r Lille 7ᵉ	(1)42 61 15 95
>>	André 44 r Lille 7ᵉ	(1)42 61 15 96
>>	André 15 r Olivier Noyer 14ᵉ	(1)45 41 28 47
>>	André 2 pass Piver 11ᵉ	(1)43 55 53 28
>>	André 35 r Popincourt 11ᵉ	(1)47 00 62 58
>>	André 6 r Prouvaires 1er	(1)42 36 22 90
>>	André 1 r Ste Lucie 15ᵉ	(1)45 75 22 05
>>	Anna 35 r Beaunier 14ᵉ	(1)45 41 37 47
>>	Anne 13 r Couronnes 20ᵉ	(1)43 58 48 32
>>	Annie 9 pl St Sulpice 6ᵉ	(1)43 29 53 21
>>	Anne-Charlotte 88 r Varenne 7ᵉ	(1)45 56 09 92
>>	Anne-Florence 10 r Cure 16ᵉ	(1)45 20 52 61
>>	Béatrice 105 r Fbg St Denis 10ᵉ	(1)45 23 13 32
>>	Béatrice 6 r Guillaume Bertrand 11ᵉ	(1)48 05 96 73
>>	Béatrice 6 r Jasmin 16ᵉ	(1)45 20 19 26
>>	Benoît 16 r Jeanne Hachette 15ᵉ	(1)42 50 00 51
>>	Benoît 19 r Liège 9ᵉ	(1)44 91 93 64
>>	Bernard 22 r Émile Dubois 14ᵉ	(1)45 65 26 61
>>	Bernard 33 av Mar Maunoury 16ᵉ	(1)45 25 12 90
>>	Bernard 4 r Oscar Roty 15ᵉ	(1)40 60 62 19
>>	Bernard 279 r Vaugirard 15ᵉ	(1)45 33 65 77
>>	Berthe 64 r Sedaine 11ᵉ	(1)47 00 55 98
>>	Bertrand 7 r Léon Delhomme 15ᵉ	(1)48 28 65 62
>>	Blanche 32 r Lille 7ᵉ	(1)42 61 14 57
>>	Brigitte 5 r Lasteyrie 16ᵉ	(1)45 00 80 26
>>	Brigitte 5 r Lasteyrie 16ᵉ	(1)45 00 97 06
>>	Bruno 7 r Abbé Groult 15ᵉ	(1)40 45 07 06
>>	Camille	
	102 r Léon Maurice Nordmann 13ᵉ	(1)45 87 36 59
>>	Carole 22 av St Ouen 18ᵉ	(1)45 22 99 18
>>	C 1 r Linné 5ᵉ	(1)43 36 33 01
>>	Catherine 15 r Trois Frères 18ᵉ	(1)42 54 72 94
>>	Cécile 22 r Cherbourg 15ᵉ	(1)45 32 98 17
>>	Cécile 86 r Cherche Midi 6ᵉ	(1)45 44 81 52
>>	Cécile 75 bd Picpus 12ᵉ	(1)43 45 97 72
>>	Cécile 122 r Raymond Losserand 14ᵉ	(1)45 43 68 66
>>	Cécile 59 bd Voltaire 11ᵉ	(1)43 55 46 71
>>	Cédric 95 r Boileau 16ᵉ	(1)40 50 72 46
>>	Céline 10 r Aristide Bruant 18ᵉ	(1)42 55 85 18
>>	Christian 14 av Bugeaud 16ᵉ	(1)47 27 31 03
>>	Christian médecin	
	127 r Caulaincourt 18ᵉ	(1)42 59 51 67
>>	Christian 6 r Filles du Calvaire 3ᵉ	(1)48 04 95 37
>>	Christiane médecin	
	42 av René Coty 14ᵉ	(1)43 27 01 78
>>	Christophe 18 r Beccaria 12ᵉ	(1)43 47 43 50
>>	Christophe 5 pass Chemin Vert 11ᵉ	(1)48 05 21 44

FABRE (suite)
>>	Christophe 119 av Jean Jaurès 19ᵉ	(1)42 40 11 77
>>	Claire 27 r Eglise 15ᵉ	(1)45 75 70 38
>>	Claire 11 r Pierre Levée 11ᵉ	(1)40 21 35 37
>>	Claire 5 r Suisses 14ᵉ	(1)40 44 75 80
>>	Clarisse 27 r Boulangers 5ᵉ	(1)43 26 71 48
>>	Claude et Françoise	
	179 bd Brune 14ᵉ	(1)45 39 31 40
>>	Claude 6 r Catulle Mendès 17ᵉ	(1)46 22 96 41
>>	Claude 11 r Cavallotti 18ᵉ	(1)43 87 47 07
>>	Claude 5 pass Chemin Vert 11ᵉ	(1)43 57 44 62
>>	Claude 94 r Clignancourt 18ᵉ	(1)42 54 70 89
>>	Claude boucherie	
	86 r Fbg St Denis 10ᵉ	(1)47 70 47 06
>>	Claude 15 r Guisarde 6ᵉ	(1)43 29 92 15
>>	C 4 r Nocard 15ᵉ	(1)45 77 28 85
>>	Claude 5 r St Ambroise 11ᵉ	(1)47 00 74 82
>>	Claudie 87 r Convention 15ᵉ	(1)45 54 15 29
>>	Claudie 4 pl Porte de Bagnolet 20ᵉ	(1)43 64 66 30
>>	Colette 14 r Le Sueur 16ᵉ	(1)45 00 23 12
>>	Colette 106 r Tour 16ᵉ	(1)45 04 87 96
>>	Coline 46 bis r Maraîchers 20ᵉ	(1)43 71 31 89
>>	Corinne Ocour	
	3 r Eugène Jumin 19ᵉ	(1)42 41 34 43
>>	Cyrille 48 r Liancourt 14ᵉ	(1)45 38 66 45
>>	Claude-Marie	
	7 r Campagne Première 14ᵉ	(1)43 21 57 09
>>	Daniel 4 r Corot 16ᵉ	(1)42 88 32 73
>>	Daniel 19 r Doct Finlay 15ᵉ	(1)45 77 05 67
>>	Daniel 9 r Duvivier 7ᵉ	(1)45 51 90 96
>>	Daniel tapiss décorat	
	9 r Duvivier 7ᵉ	(1)47 05 37 08
>>	Daniel 11 r Figuier 4ᵉ	(1)42 77 48 32
>>	Daniel 29 r Ponthieu 8ᵉ	(1)43 59 54 80
>>	Daniel 37 r St Fargeau 20ᵉ	(1)43 63 54 95
>>	Futur Numéro	(1)40 30 54 95
>>	Danièle infirmier BAT COUR	
	13 r Rivoli 4ᵉ	(1)48 04 08 83
>>	David 5 villa Croix Nivert 15ᵉ	(1)47 83 27 84
>>	Delphine 106 r Vieille du Temple 3ᵉ	(1)48 04 71 42
>>	Denise	
	14 r Chevalier de La Barre 18ᵉ	(1)42 23 53 02
>>	Denyse 9 bis bd Rochechouart 9ᵉ	(1)48 78 72 59
>>	Didier 4 r Orsel 18ᵉ	(1)42 59 38 13
>>	Dominique 100 r Amsterdam 9ᵉ	(1)44 53 02 25
>>	Dominique 130 r Chemin Vert 11ᵉ	(1)43 55 47 74
>>	Dominique 19 r Ducouédic 14ᵉ	(1)43 27 76 16
>>	Dominique	
	206 r Fbg St Antoine 12ᵉ	(1)40 09 01 05
>>	Dominique 73 av Ledru Rollin 12ᵉ	(1)43 41 11 26
>>	Edmond 27 r Meuniers 12ᵉ	(1)43 07 68 38
>>	Eliane 5 sq Desaix 15ᵉ	(1)45 77 20 38
>>	Elisabeth 7 r Lacaze 14ᵉ	(1)45 45 94 67
>>	Elise 10 r Jouvenet 16ᵉ	(1)45 20 52 98
>>	Emeric 7 r Arsonval 15ᵉ	(1)43 22 73 56
>>	Emile 3 r Henri Ranvier 11ᵉ	(1)43 67 71 79
>>	Emile 34 r Plantes 14ᵉ	(1)45 40 45 70
>>	E 21 all Louise Labé 19ᵉ	(1)42 00 04 10
>>	Emmanuel	
	26 r Pont Louis Philippe 4ᵉ	(1)48 04 59 89
>>	Emmanuelle 139 r Longchamp 16ᵉ	(1)40 72 64 63
>>	Emmanuelle 123 r Université 7ᵉ	(1)45 51 38 92
>>	Eric 10 r Augustin Thierry 19ᵉ	(1)42 39 30 30

FABRE Erick fleuriste
—	52 r St Dominique 7ᵉ	(1)45 55 71 84
—	Télécopieur	(1)45 55 80 81

FABRE Fabienne masseur kinesi
	86 av Daumesnil 12ᵉ	(1)43 42 91 12
>>	Fabienne 96 av Daumesnil 12ᵉ	(1)44 75 35 06
>>	Fernande 58 r Py 20ᵉ	(1)43 61 13 81
>>	Florence architecture	
	7 pass Étienne Delaunay 11ᵉ	(1)43 56 66 30

1. What is Alice Fabre's telephone number?

    _____

2. What is Coline Fabre's telephone number? Write it out using French words.

    _____

3. How many people named Cécile Fabre live in Paris?

    _____

4. What is Florence Fabre's occupation?

    _____

5. What is Albert Fabre's car phone number?

    _____

6. In what district of Paris does Annie Fabre live?

    _____

7. What is Erick Fabre's fax number?

    _____

8. What is Anna Fabre's street address?

    _____

9. How many different telephone numbers does Brigitte Fabre have?

    _____

10. What will Daniel Fabre's new telephone number be?

    _____

Unit 5

A Match the product in column B with the city from which it comes in column A.

A		B
1. Reims	_____	a) cotton and linen
2. Bordeaux	_____	b) tires
3. Lille	_____	c) champagne
4. Strasbourg	_____	d) silk
5. Lyon	_____	e) red wine
6. Clermont-Ferrand	_____	f) "pâté de foie gras"

B After studying the map in your textbook and reading the information on page 28, answer each question by circling the correct river.

1. Which river empties into "la Manche"?

    a) Garonne   b) Rhine   c) Seine

2. Which river starts as a stream fed by a Swiss glacier?

    a) Loire   b) Rhône   c) Garonne

3. Which river is a famous tourist attraction?

    a) Rhône   b) Garonne   c) Loire

4. Which river flows through the city of Paris?

    a) Rhine   b) Loire   c) Seine

5. Which river has its source in the Pyrenees Mountains?

    a) Seine   b) Garonne   c) Rhine

6. Which river divides France and Germany?

    a) Rhine   b) Rhône   c) Seine

C Which expression doesn't belong with the others? Circle the letter of the misfit.

1. a) Bordeaux b) Strasbourg c) Rhône

2. a) Suisse b) Lyon c) Espagne

3. a) Seine b) océan Atlantique c) Manche

4. a) les Alpes b) Le Havre c) les Pyrénées

5. a) Rouen b) Garonne c) Loire

D Study the map in your textbook to tell the direction you must take as you travel from one city to another. Choose from the following directions: N (north), NE (northeast), S (south), SE (southeast), E (east), NW (northwest), W (west), SW (southwest).

FROM	TO	DIRECTION
1. Lyon	Marseille	_____
2. Bordeaux	Strasbourg	_____
3. Paris	Le Havre	_____
4. Rouen	Reims	_____
5. Lyon	Clermont-Ferrand	_____
6. Lille	Bordeaux	_____

E Using the map on page 27 of your textbook as a model, draw your own map of France. Label the ten cities, five rivers and two mountain ranges you have studied.

F   Circle the following countries, cities and bodies of water in the letter grid. The letters may go forward or backward; they may go up, down, across or diagonally.

1. France
2. Biarritz
3. Rouen
4. Lille
5. Lyon
6. Paris
7. Reims
8. Strasbourg
9. Bordeaux
10. Seine
11. Loire
12. Rhône
13. Rhin
14. océan Atlantique
15. mer Méditerranée
16. Espagne
17. Italie
18. Allemagne
19. Suisse
20. Metz

```
                    R I E L O H T S M L A
                    A K I G N F Z E E H C
                    E L R A B O N I D I O
                    L U S D D C A P I G N
        E K N L J E O M A I F E Z A X U A E D R O B I
        B N Y A D B A L L E M A G N E G J T A N H G E
        I O X P S A N I K P O N W I M Z T I R R A I B
        N I F A O D L G N E B A C H O N D N O Q S H N
        H X R V M E R M E D I T E R R A N E E L U F I
        V T A I Y H A N O I W L O Y S S Z E P V I P D
        S Z N M O I R E F Z A A N H A P M T T F S L A
        R K C N A M E S P A G N E I T A L I E I S O J
        G O E L M W C I E G K T A G N E S L E M E A G
        S H M E T I E A J O V I H R E D E S L R E P S
                    P R A I L Q O I R N I
                    A D I R O U E N A R F
                    E N Y O T E S M A E T
                    J G S M L O N P E R I
```

G   Imagine that you go to a travel agency to inquire about a trip to France. Your partner plays the role of the travel agent. Ask the agent about what cities you should visit and what you should see while you're there. Depending on your interests, plan your itinerary with the travel agent for a two-week trip. Then reverse roles so that your partner is the traveler. Come up with a different itinerary to fit your partner's interests.

H Imagine that you are taking a trip to Lyon, one of the fastest-growing and largest cities in France. Your guidebook has a listing of selected hotels and their location in the city. Use this information to answer the questions that follow. You will need to know some new words: *métro* (subway), *chbres* (rooms, abbreviation for *chambres*), *centre commercial* (shopping center) and *gare* (train station).

LYON

NOTRE SÉLECTION D'HÔTELS

CATÉG.	CODE	NOM DE L'HÔTEL	HÔTEL 🍴	Nbre Chbres	PLAN	CHAMBRE ☎	TV	Confort
11	181101	LES RELAIS BLEUS	●	86	1	●	●	BWC
	181102	CAMPANILE PERRACHE	●	108	2	●	●	DBW
	181103	DE LA CROIX ROUSSE		34	3	●	●	DWC
21	182101	AXOTEL PERRACHE	●	130	4	●	●	DBW
	182102	DE CREQUI		28	5	●	●	BWC
	182103	BRISTOL	●	113	6	●	●	DWC
	182104	CAMPANILE PART DIEU	●	169	7	●	●	BWC
	182106	LUTETIA COMFORT INN		60	8	●	●	DBW
31	183102	CONCORDE	●	140	9	●	●	DBW
	183103	CARLTON		87	10	●	●	BWC
41	184101	LA COUR DES LOGES	●	63	11	●	●	BWC

1. What are the names of the two rivers that flow through Lyon?

    _____

2. Which of the listed hotels has the most rooms?

    _____

3. Which hotel is the smallest?

    _____

4. Which hotels do not have a TV and a telephone in the rooms?

    _____

5. Which hotels do not have restaurants?

    _____

6. Which hotel would you choose if you wanted to be near the Part-Dieu shopping center?

    _____

7. If you wanted to be in a hotel that was near a subway station, would you choose the Bristol or the Concorde?

    _____

8. If you wanted to be near the train station, would you choose the Carlton or the Axotel Perrache?

    _____

Unit 6

A

Match each French expression in column B with its corresponding description in column A.

	A		B
1.	Where the kings and queens of France used to live.	_____	a) immeuble
			b) W.-C.
2.	The room where food is prepared.	_____	c) salle de bains
			d) château
3.	An apartment building.	_____	e) maison individuelle
4.	What you might go on a camping trip in.	_____	f) caravane
			g) cuisine
5.	The room with the bathtub or shower.	_____	
6.	The room with the toilet.	_____	
7.	A single-family home.	_____	

B

What might you find in a *salon*? Circle the appropriate items.

mur	immeuble	bibliothèque	livre
jardin	salle de classe	craie	château
chaise	corbeille à papier	roulotte	appartement
maison	horloge	peinture	W.-C.

C Which expression is an appropriate answer to the question? Circle the letter of the correct answer.

1. Où est le garage?

   a) Dans la maison.

   b) Là-bas.

   c) Cinq pièces.

2. Où habite Maryvonne?

   a) Maryvonne habite dans une pièce.

   b) Maryvonne habite dans un appartement.

   c) Maryvonne habite dans le jardin.

3. Où est le jardin?

   a) Derrière la maison.

   b) Dans la maison.

   c) Dans le garage.

4. Où est la tente?

   a) Dans le jardin.

   b) Dans la salle de bains.

   c) Derrière le taille-crayon.

5. Tu habites dans un appartement?

   a) Oui, dans une hutte.

   b) Oui, dans un immeuble.

   c) Oui, dans une maison individuelle.

D Draw a diagram or floor plan of your house or apartment. Label the rooms in French.

E Unscramble the words.

1. reggaa   _____

2. petaramtepn   _____

3. thetu   _____

4. cipee   _____

5. sucieni   _____

6. etnet   _____

7. nasol   _____

8. mehrcab   _____

Nom: _____ Date: _____

F Find your way through the maze to your bed. As you trace your way beginning at the
entrance arrow, list in French each type of house or shelter you encounter.

_____

_____

_____

_____

_____

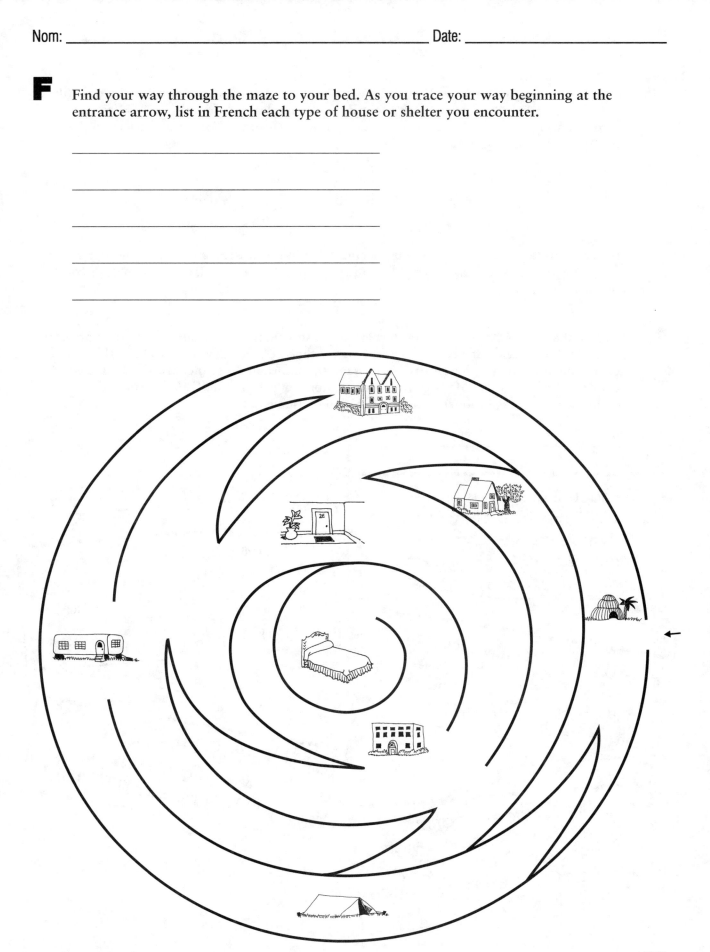

G Imagine that you've just moved into a new house. Your friend comes to visit and would like a tour. He or she asks you where each room is. For example, your friend says "*Où est la cuisine?*" You point out the kitchen and say "*Voilà la cuisine.*" Your friend asks you the location of the following rooms:

la chambre	les W.-C.
le salon	la salle de bains
la cuisine	la salle à manger

He or she may also ask about the garage and the yard (*le garage, le jardin*). After you point out all the locations, reverse roles. This time you ask where these places are and your friend points them out.

H Imagine that you are going to move to Paris for a short time. You want to rent an apartment, so you look through some classified ads. Answer the questions that follow about the apartments identified by letters. To understand the information in the ads, you will need to know some new words: *M°* (subway, abbreviation for *métro*), *meublé(e)* (furnished), *m²* (square meters), *étage* (floor), *mois* (month), *août* (August).

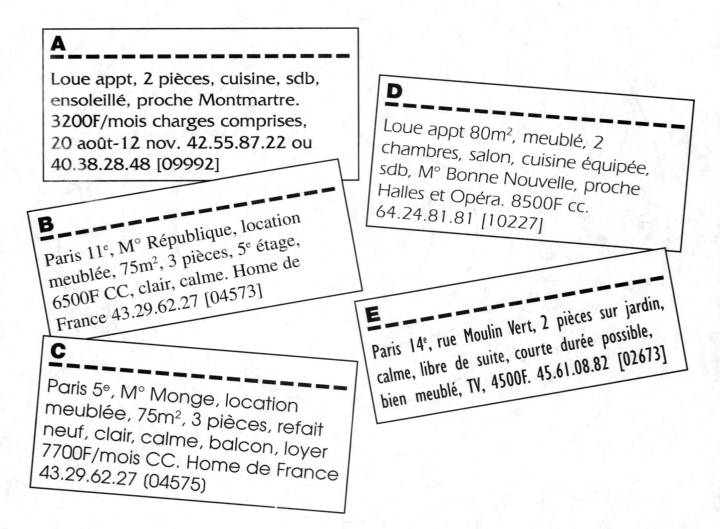

A

Loue appt, 2 pièces, cuisine, sdb, ensoleillé, proche Montmartre. 3200F/mois charges comprises, 20 août-12 nov. 42.55.87.22 ou 40.38.28.48 [09992]

B

Paris 11ᵉ, M° République, location meublée, 75m², 3 pièces, 5ᵉ étage, 6500F CC, clair, calme. Home de France 43.29.62.27 [04573]

C

Paris 5ᵉ, M° Monge, location meublée, 75m², 3 pièces, refait neuf, clair, calme, balcon, loyer 7700F/mois CC. Home de France 43.29.62.27 (04575)

D

Loue appt 80m², meublé, 2 chambres, salon, cuisine équipée, sdb, M° Bonne Nouvelle, proche Halles et Opéra. 8500F cc. 64.24.81.81 [10227]

E

Paris 14ᵉ, rue Moulin Vert, 2 pièces sur jardin, calme, libre de suite, courte durée possible, bien meublé, TV, 4500F. 45.61.08.82 [02673]

1. In what district of Paris is apartment E located?

   _____

2. What is the closest subway station to apartment B?

   _____

3. Are all five of the apartments furnished?

   _____

4. How many rooms does apartment D have? What are they?

   _____

   _____

5. How large in meters is apartment B?

   _____

6. On what floor is apartment B located?

   _____

7. When can you rent apartment A?

   _____

8. What does apartment E look out on?

   _____

9. What is the monthly rent in francs for apartment C? If there are five francs to the dollar, what is the monthly rent in dollars?

   _____

   _____

10. According to the advertisements, which three apartments would be very quiet?

    _____

Unit 7

A   Which word doesn't belong with the others? Circle the letter of the word whose gender (masculine or feminine) is different from the others.

1.   a)   nièce   b)   tante   c)   neveu

2.   a)   père   b)   sœur   c)   oncle

3.   a)   femme   b)   frère   c)   grand-mère

4.   a)   petite-fille   b)   fils   c)   cousin

5.   a)   parrain   b)   oncle   c)   fille

B   Complete each sentence by circling the name of the correct family member.

1.   Ma mère et mon père sont mes....

     a)   parents

     b)   enfants

     c)   fils

2.   La fille de mes parents est ma....

     a)   cousine

     b)   sœur

     c)   frère

3.   La mère de mon père est ma....

     a)   marraine

     b)   petite-fille

     c)   grand-mère

4.   Le frère de ma mère est mon....

     a)   père

     b)   neveu

     c)   oncle

5.   La sœur de mon cousin est ma....

     a)   tante

     b)   cousine

     c)   nièce

6.   La mère de mon neveu est ma....

     a)   sœur

     b)   cousine

     c)   nièce

C Draw your own family tree. Start at the bottom by writing your name and the names of any brothers or sisters. Then, beside each person's name, write his or her relationship to you (for example, *Robert, mon frère*). Next, show your parents, their siblings, their parents, etc.

D Using the short composition in Activity H on page 49 of your textbook as a model, write a composition in French about your own family. Tell where your family lives, if your family is large or small and how many people are in your family. Then tell the names and ages of any brothers or sisters. Finally, tell if you live in a house or an apartment.

Ma famille

_____

_____

_____

_____

_____

_____

_____

_____

_____

_____

E Create a collage of pictures in which you show an interesting, imaginary family. Be as creative as you can in finding pictures of well-known people who would compose an interesting and perhaps humorous family. You may want to look for these pictures in back issues of magazines or newspapers, or you may decide to draw pictures of this imaginary family. Then take your pictures and arrange them in a collage. Label each person with his or her name and family relationship (for example, *Bill Clinton, le père*).

F Mots croisés

Vertical

1. My brother.
2. Also.
3. «Ta mère et...père, sont-ils ici?»
4. «Mon père et...frères sont dans le jardin.»
5. Boy.
6. «La sœur de Denise s'appelle....»
8. Family.
12. And.
15. Baby.
18. «Denise, Jeanne et Patrice sont les...de Bernard.»
19. «Le frère de Denise s'appelle....»
20. «Jeanne est la...de Denise.»
25. «La sœur de ma mère est ma....»
26. Husband.
27. Their.

Horizontal

1. Godmother.
7. The children.
9. «André et...femme sont à la réunion.»
10. «...est-ce?»
11. Mother.
13. «...père, tel fils.»
14. «...est un oncle de Michel et de Constance.»
16. «Le père de Jacques s'appelle....»
17. Uncle.
19. Relatives, parents.
21. «Le parrain de...est sur la terrasse.»
22. «Qu'est-ce...c'est?»
23. «Ta sœur et...frères sont là-bas.»
24. Grandson.
28. «...mère et mon père sont à Lyon.»
29. «Hervé est l'oncle de....»
30. "Bien...."
31. «Ton neveu et...nièce s'appellent Michel et Constance.»
32. Daughter.
33. Niece.

G Bring to class a family photo showing as many of your relatives as possible. (If you can't find a photo, you may draw a picture of your relatives. You might choose to bring a picture of your imaginary family from the back issue of a magazine or newspaper.) Your partner will ask you who each person is. After you answer, your partner will ask you the name of each person.

> EXAMPLE: Your partner asks: Qui est-ce?
> You answer: C'est ma tante.
>
> Your partner asks: Comment s'appelle-t-elle?
> You answer: Elle s'appelle Claire.

Then reverse roles. This time you ask about your partner's family members.

H In some French newspapers you will find a section titled *le carnet du jour* where various family-related news items are reported. Use the information in these short articles to answer the following questions. You will need to know some new words: *naissances* (births), *fiançailles* (engagements), *deuils* (deaths).

le carnet du jour

naissances

**Pierre ALBOUY
et Mathilde**, née Voyer, et leur fille Camille sont heureux de vous annoncer la naissance de
Laure
le 8 juillet.
**M. Henri d'AVOUT
et Mme**, née Sabine de Laage de Bellefaye, sont heureux d'annoncer la naissance de leur 22e petit-enfant
Charlotte d'AVOUT
sœur de Geoffroy, Christophe et Matthieu, le 14 juillet, chez **Nicolas et Isabelle** née Curie.

fiançailles

M. Serge ALEXIS
et Mme, née Joëlle Dervillée,
M. Jean-François LIMOUZI
et Mme, née Françoise Richard, sont heureux d'annoncer les fiançailles de leurs enfants
Elodie et Guillaume
Le Puy. Lyon.

mariages

**M. et Mme Henri
BORGET
M. et Mme Serge
LECOMTE**
sont heureux d'annoncer le mariage de leurs enfants
Catherine et Eric
le samedi 17 juillet, à 16 h 30, en l'église Saint-Martin d'Ermenonville (Oise).

deuils

Mme Michèle Barré, son épouse, Josquin et Brigitte, ses enfants, ses parents et ses amis ont la douleur de vous faire part du décès de
Martin BARRÉ
survenu le 8 juillet, à l'âge de 68 ans. La cérémonie religieuse aura lieu le mardi 13 juillet, à 11 heures, au cimetière du Montparnasse, entrée principale, 3 boulevard Edgar-Quinet, Paris (14e).

1. What are the full names of the engaged couple?

   _____

2. Who passed away on July 8?

   _____

3. How old was he when he died?

   _____

4. How many children did he have? What are their names?

   _____

   _____

5. What are the names of the bride's parents?

   _____

6. What did Monsieur and Madame Albouy name their new child?

   _____

7. Are there any other children in the Albouy family?

   _____

8. Monsieur and Madame Henri d'Avout announce the birth of Charlotte d'Avout. What is Charlotte's relationship to Monsieur and Madame Henri d'Avout?

   _____

9. Is Charlotte their first grandchild?

   _____

10. How many brothers does Charlotte have? What are their names?

   _____

   _____

Unit 8

A Circle the letter of the correct answer to each question.

1. Who mainly works with his or her hands?

   a) professeur   b) plombier

2. Who generally works outside?

   a) fermier   b) cuisinière

3. Who generally works inside?

   a) commerçante   b) facteur

4. Who generally is paid by the hour?

   a) artiste   b) mécanicien

5. Who works in front of a group of people?

   a) charpentier   b) actrice

6. Who generally would come to your house to perform his or her service?

   a) médecin   b) électricien

Nom: _____ Date: _____

B Circle the letter of the course offering most closely associated with each occupation.

1. médecin

    a) science   b) economics   c) woodworking

2. musicienne

    a) geography   b) history   c) music

3. fermier

    a) art   b) agriculture   c) literature

4. commerçante

    a) gymnastics   b) automotive engineering   c) marketing

5. cuisinier

    a) nutrition   b) computer science c) geometry

6. acteur

    a) drama   b) biology   c) Italian

C Certain occupations require special skills. Match the talent or skill in column B with the job in which you would use that skill in column A.

A	B
1. mécanicienne _____	a) Has a good sense of rhythm.
2. cuisinier _____	b) Knows how and when to plant crops.
3. électricien _____	c) Can help you keep healthy.
4. charpentier _____	d) Has a good sense of color, design and perspective.
5. médecin _____	e) Knows how to fix an engine.
6. actrice _____	f) Can create appetizing dishes.
7. musicienne _____	g) Can portray convincingly a variety of characters.
8. plombier _____	h) Knows hard wood from soft wood.
9. fermière _____	i) Knows how to wire a house.
10. artiste _____	j) Can repair a leaky faucet.

D List in French the people who could help you in the following activities.

1. Three people who could help you build a house:

   _____   _____

   _____

2. A person who could help you find what you need in a store:

   _____

3. Two people who could help you recover when you're ill:

   _____   _____

4. A person who could help you stay in touch with your pen pal:

   _____

5. Two people who could entertain you in the theater and the concert hall:

   _____   _____

6. A person who could teach you history or science:

   _____

E Unscramble the words.

1. ratcue   _____

2. meniferiri   _____

3. tasteir   _____

4. erpusoserf   _____

5. catfure   _____

6. icumsine   _____

7. therapernic _____

8. bermopil   _____

F Mots croisés

Vertical

1. Harrison Ford's profession.
2. "Bureau...placement."
5. «Monsieur Diouf...professeur.»
6. «...fais-tu?»
8. «Il y a combien de pièces dans ta...?»
9. Artist.
10. Julia Child's profession.
13. Actress.
14. «...est ta profession?»
15. Guaranteed.
16. Bruce Springsteen's profession.
19. «Que...tu?»
22. «Où sont ton...et ta mère?»
23. Husband.
25. «Où sont...garages?»
26. «Quelle est...profession?»

Horizontal

3. Doctor.
4. He manages a farm.
7. He manages a store.
9. The same as 13 down.
11. «...est-ce?»
12. Letter carrier.
17. «Je...artiste.»
18. Work, employment.
20. «Pierre...Jean-Marc sont musiciens.»
21. Carpenter.
24. A boy's name.
27. He repairs cars.

Nom: _____ Date: _____

G With a partner play "What's My Line?" in French. Pick one of the occupations whose French name you have learned. Then think of as many French words as you can that have something to do with this occupation. Say these words as clues for your partner, who tries to guess your occupation.

EXAMPLE: You say: craie, bureau, salle de classe
You say: Your partner asks: Es-tu professeur?
You say: Oui, je suis professeur.

Then reverse roles. This time your partner gives you clues and you guess his or her occupation.

H Here are some classified ads from various newspapers in French-speaking countries. The ads are placed either by firms that are hiring or by people that are looking for jobs. Answer the questions that follow using the information in the ads. You will need to know some new words: *J. H.* (young man, abbreviation for *jeune homme*), *cherche* or *recherche* (is looking for), *ans* (years old), *cours d'anglais* (English courses).

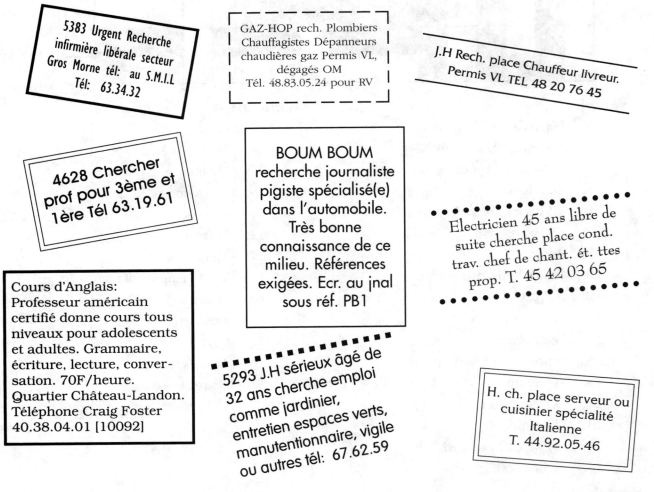

1. Is a man or a woman looking for work as a gardener? How old is this person?

   _____

2. What is the telephone number of the organization that is looking for a nurse?

   _____

3. What is the nationality of the teacher who is offering to give English courses? What is the teacher's name?

   _____

4. For what age groups are these English courses intended?

   _____

5. How many francs per hour does the teacher charge?

   _____

6. What is the telephone number of the organization that is looking for a teacher?

   _____

7. Is a man or a woman looking for work as a cook?

   _____

8. What ethnic style of cooking does this person specialize in?

   _____

9. The magazine *BOUM BOUM* is looking for a journalist. In what area should the journalist specialize?

   _____

10. How old is the electrician who is looking for work? What is his telephone number?

    _____

11. What company is looking for plumbers?

    _____

12. What is the telephone number of the person looking for work as a chauffeur?

    _____

Unit 9

A You are hungry. Circle the items that will satisfy your hunger.

pain   **bifteck**   sel

                              soucoupe

                  poire

serviette

                      faim   poulet

        cuiller

œufs   pomme   nappe

B You are thirsty. Circle the items that will quench your thirst.

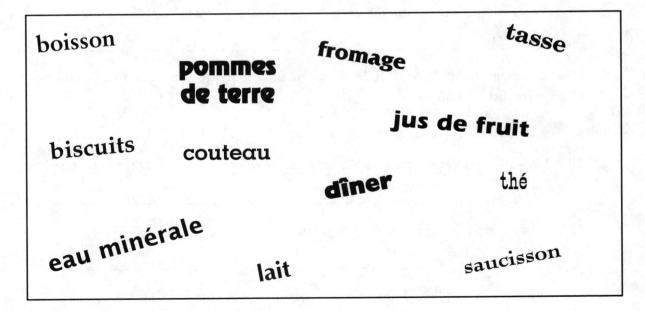

boisson   fromage   **tasse**

        **pommes
        de terre**

                                      jus de fruit

biscuits   couteau

                          dîner   thé

eau minérale

                    lait   saucisson

C Match the French expression in column B with its corresponding description in column A.

A		B
1. The seasoning some people put on french fries.	_____	a) beurre
		b) sucre
2. What you spread on bread.	_____	c) petit déjeuner
3. What you drink milk from.	_____	d) nappe
4. What you add to sweeten something.	_____	e) verre
		f) tasse
5. What you cut meat with.	_____	g) cuiller
6. What you drink coffee from.	_____	h) sel
7. The first meal of the day.	_____	i) couteau
8. What you eat soup with.	_____	
9. What covers the table.	_____	

D Circle the letter of the correct answer to each question.

1. Which French city is famous for its fish chowder?

   a) Le Havre   b) Marseille   c) Lyon

2. What French delicacy is a kind of shellfish?

   a) "pot au feu"   b) "canard à l'orange"   c) "escargots"

3. For which part of the meal would you serve "coq au vin"?

   a) beverage   b) dessert   c) main dish

4. Which area of France is known for its egg custard pastry?

   a) Provence   b) Lorraine   c) Loire River valley

5. What is used to make "crêpes suzette"?

   a) pancakes   b) roast duck   c) chicken broth

6. What is a specialty from the city of Strasbourg?

   a) liver pâté   b) soup   c) snails

E To keep in good shape, you should have a balanced diet. Each day you should eat at least two servings from these five food groups:

        Group 1:   milk, yogurt and cheese
        Group 2:   vegetables
        Group 3:   fruits
        Group 4:   meat, poultry, fish, dry beans, eggs and nuts
        Group 5:   bread, cereal, rice and pasta

For each category, name at least two French foods or specialties from pages 56 to 58 in your textbook that will fulfill these daily requirements.

Group 1: _____

_____

Group 2: _____

_____

Group 3: _____

_____

Group 4: _____

_____

Group 5: _____

_____

F   Unscramble the words.

1. sibnoos   _____

2. cutrhtefoe _____

3. juenreed   _____

4. miaf   _____

5. ganmer   _____

6. bamojn   _____

7. lagec   _____

8. evirpo   _____

9. ompem   _____

10. unicsei   _____

G   With your partner draw on other paper pictures of the foods, beverages and tableware whose French names you have learned. Instead of drawing you may choose to find pictures of these items in back issues of magazines or newspapers. Then cut out these pictures. Take turns with your partner showing a picture as your partner identifies it. Alternate showing and naming objects until all pictures are identified. See who can name the most items correctly.

EXAMPLE: Your partner shows you a picture of a pineapple.
You say: ananas

H Imagine that you are grocery shopping at the Shopi store in France. After you examine a section of their weekly specials, answer the questions that follow. You will need to know some new words: *côte de bœuf* (beef roast), *blanc* (white), *kg* (abbreviation for *kilogramme*), *tranches* (slices), *pamplemousse* (grapefruit), *litre* (liter).

CRÈME GLACÉE
MENTHE
AVEC COPEAUX DE CHOCOLAT
PLEIN SOURIRE
1 LITRE

GLACE TOUS PARFUMS
Plein Sourire
le litre
12F95

VIEUX PANÉ

VIEUX PANE *
50% M.G.
le kg
55F80

KERGAL KERGAL KERGAL
Jus de pamplemousse   Jus d'orange   Jus d'orange
LE MEILLEUR DU FRUIT

JUS D'ORANGE ou JUS DE PAMPLEMOUSSE
Kergal
la brik de 1 litre
9F90

10 SAUCISSES DE STRASBOURG
Fumées au bois de hêtre
BOCADOU

SAUCISSES DE STRASBOURG
Bocadou
le paquet de 10 - 350 g soit le kg : 25.71 F
9F00

BOCADOU
JAMBON
SURCHOIX
avec couenne
tranche charcutière

JAMBON SURCHOIX
Bocadou
les 4 tranches - 200 g
soit le kg : 49.00 F
9F80

NOUVEAU

DANONE
SALADE de FRUITS FRAIS
DANONE
SALADE de FRUITS FRAIS
FRESH FRUITS SALAD

SALADE DE FRUITS FRAIS
Danone
les 2×175 g
soit le kg : 25.57 F
8F95

LE GAULOIS
BLANC de POULET
Cuit. Traité en Salaison
4 TRANCHES
180 g

BLANC DE POULET FAÇON JAMBON
Le Gaulois
les 4 tranches - 180 g
soit le kg : 80.56 F
14F50

COTE DE BŒUF *
le kg
59F80

shopi

1. What four kinds of meat or poultry are on special this week?

   _____

2. How much in francs does one kilogram of beef cost? If there are five francs to the dollar and 2.2 kilograms to the pound, how much in dollars does one pound of beef cost?

   _____

   _____

3. How many slices of ham do you get for 9F 80?

   _____

4. How many sausages do you get for nine francs?

   _____

5. What two kinds of fruit juice are on special?

   _____

6. By what unit of measurement is ice cream sold?

   _____

7. How many individual servings of fruit salad do you get for 8F 95?

   _____

8. How much in francs does one kilogram of cheese cost?

   _____

9. If you had to select three of these items for your dinner tonight, which ones would you choose?

   _____

   _____

Unit 10

A Complete each sentence by writing the name of the appropriate artist.

1. If you like blurry images, you might like the paintings by

    _____ .

2. If you like realistic images, you might like the paintings by

    _____ .

3. If you like a scene showing action, you might like the paintings by

    _____ .

4. If you like paintings based on historical figures, you might like the paintings by

    _____ .

5. If you like paintings that show contrasting colors, you might like the paintings by

    _____ .

6. If you like paintings that show the blending of colors, you might like the paintings by

    _____ .

B Match the artists in column B with the appropriate expressions in column A.

	A			**B**
1.	*Fantasia arabe*	_____	a)	Jacques Louis David
2.	*The Croquet Match*	_____	b)	Eugène Delacroix
3.	*The Death of Socrates*	_____	c)	Édouard Manet
4.	*On the Beach*	_____		
5.	impressionism	_____		
6.	neoclassicism	_____		
7.	romanticism	_____		
8.	clear lines	_____		
9.	fuzzy lines	_____		
10.	flowing lines	_____		
11.	importance of feelings	_____		
12.	importance of form	_____		
13.	importance of impressions	_____		
14.	1798-1863	_____		
15.	1832-83	_____		
16.	1748-1825	_____		

C Having read about the lives, paintings and artistic styles of David, Delacroix and Manet on page 63 of your textbook, decide which artist fits each description.

1. He spent time in North Africa. Some of his paintings reflect this exotic influence.

   _____

2. He tended to paint scenes of contemporary, everyday life.

   _____

3. He took an active part in the French Revolution.

   _____

4. He and his followers treated spacial relationships in an innovative way.

   _____

5. He studied art in Italy.

   _____

6. He opposed the static paintings of the neoclassical school.

   _____

7. His painting of *The Balcony* inspired other painters to also work outdoors.

   _____

8. He expressed his passions in visible form.

   _____

9. He glorified the reign of Napoleon in his paintings.

   _____

D You have just learned about three different schools (or styles) of art: neoclassical, romantic and impressionistic. Now it's your turn to show some artistic creativity. On other paper make three drawings, as simple or as detailed as your talents allow. Each should be representative of one of the three artistic movements. The first drawing (neoclassical) should be an official portrait of George Washington. The second one (romantic) should be a drawing of a ferocious tiger. The third one (impressionistic) should be a picture of a sunset over a lake.

E Unscramble the words. They are either names of the artists or English names of the schools (or styles) of art described in this unit.

1. tarminoc _____

2. radixcelo _____

3. seinpoismirms _____

4. atmen _____

5. vaddi _____

6. salliconaces _____

F Of the four pictures you have studied in this unit, *The Death of Socrates, Fantasia arabe, The Croquet Match* and *On the Beach*, decide which one is your favorite. Your teacher will designate each corner of your classroom as one of these four paintings. Go to the corner that represents your favorite picture. Pair up with a partner. Each of you tells the other why you like this painting the best. Then get together with another pair of students in your corner so that you can tell the new pair why your partner prefers this painting. Finally, a spokesperson from each of the four groups tells the entire class why students from that group prefer that picture.

G Mots croisés

Vertical

1. Jacques Louis....
2. The use of...to show feeling was important to Delacroix.
4. "..., autres mœurs."
6. David won the...de Rome.
8. *The Croquet....*
9. Manet's teacher was Thomas....
10. David's paintings show...themes.
11. A painting by Delacroix.
14. «Quelle est...profession?»
18. An impressionist painter.
19. A seasoning you put on popcorn.
21. Delacroix used flowing lines to show....
24. "Coq...vin" is a French culinary specialty.
26. «Robert est...oncle.»

Horizontal

3. *The...of Socrates.*
5. The emperor of France.
7. The school of painters after the neoclassical school.
12. He studied under Guérin.
13. Painters study....
15. «...-tu faim?»
16. A painting by Manet.
17. Manet was one of the founders of....
20. «J'...soif.»
22. «J'ai deux tantes et deux....»
23. *The Death of....*
25. You write on the "..." with "un bâton de craie."
27. «Ce sont...mes cousins.»
28. The capital of France.
29. ...Manet.
30. ...Delacroix.

H Paris is well known for all its art museums where you can examine paintings and sculptures dating from prehistoric times to the present. Using the information from descriptions of some famous Parisian art museums, answer the questions that follow. You will need to know some new words: *siècle* (century), *nymphéas* (water lilies).

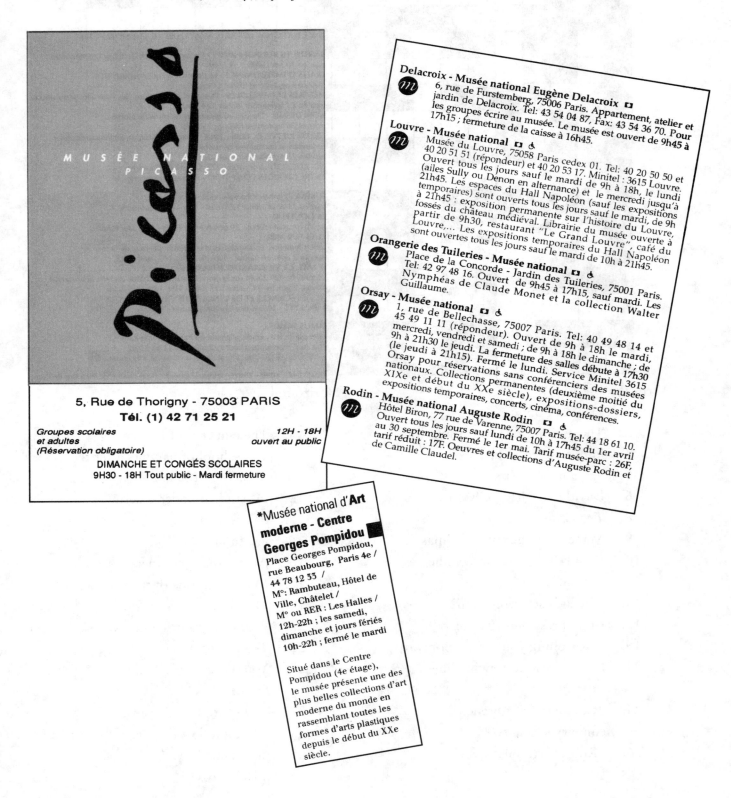

MUSÉE NATIONAL PICASSO

5, Rue de Thorigny - 75003 PARIS
Tél. (1) 42 71 25 21

Groupes scolaires   12H - 18H
et adultes   *ouvert au public*
(Réservation obligatoire)

DIMANCHE ET CONGÉS SCOLAIRES
9H30 - 18H Tout public - Mardi fermeture

Delacroix - Musée national Eugène Delacroix ▢
6, rue de Furstemberg, 75006 Paris. Appartement, atelier et jardin de Delacroix. Tel: 43 54 04 87, Fax: 43 54 36 70. Pour les groupes écrire au musée. Le musée est ouvert de 9h45 à 17h15 ; fermeture de la caisse à 16h45.

Louvre - Musée national ▢ &
Musée du Louvre, 75058 Paris cedex 01. Tel: 40 20 50 50 et 40 20 51 51 (répondeur) et 40 20 53 17. Minitel : 3615 Louvre. Ouvert tous les jours sauf le mardi de 9h à 18h, le lundi (ailes Sully ou Denon en alternance) et le mercredi jusqu'à 21h45. Les espaces du Hall Napoléon (sauf les expositions temporaires) sont ouverts tous les jours sauf le mardi, de 9h à 21h45 : exposition permanente sur l'histoire du Louvre, fossés du château médiéval. Librairie du musée, ouverte à partir de 9h30, restaurant "Le Grand Louvre", café du Louvre,... Les expositions temporaires du Hall Napoléon sont ouvertes tous les jours sauf le mardi de 10h à 21h45.

Orangerie des Tuileries - Musée national ▢ &
Place de la Concorde - Jardin des Tuileries, 75001 Paris. Tel: 42 97 48 16. Ouvert de 9h45 à 17h15, sauf mardi. Les Nymphéas de Claude Monet et la collection Walter Guillaume.

Orsay - Musée national ▢ &
1, rue de Bellechasse, 75007 Paris. Tel: 40 49 48 14 et 45 49 11 11 (répondeur). Ouvert de 9h à 18h le mardi, mercredi, vendredi et samedi ; de 9h à 18h le dimanche ; 9h à 21h30 le jeudi. La fermeture des salles débute à 17h30 (le jeudi à 21h15). Fermé le lundi. Service Minitel 3615 Orsay pour réservations sans conférenciers des musées nationaux. Collections permanentes (deuxième moitié du XIXe et début du XXe siècle), expositions-dossiers, expositions temporaires, concerts, cinema, conférences.

Rodin - Musée national Auguste Rodin &
Hôtel Biron, 77 rue de Varenne, 75007 Paris. Tel: 44 18 61 10. Ouvert tous les jours sauf lundi de 10h à 17h45 du 1er avril au 30 septembre. Fermé le 1er mai. Tarif musée-parc : 26F, tarif réduit : 17F. Oeuvres et collections d'Auguste Rodin et de Camille Claudel.

*Musée national d'Art moderne - Centre Georges Pompidou
Place Georges Pompidou, rue Beaubourg, Paris 4e /
44 78 12 33 /
M°: Rambuteau, Hôtel de Ville, Châtelet /
M° ou RER : Les Halles /
12h-22h ; les samedi, dimanche et jours fériés 10h-22h ; fermé le mardi

Situé dans le Centre Pompidou (4e étage), le musée présente une des plus belles collections d'art moderne du monde en rassemblant toutes les formes d'arts plastiques depuis le début du XXe siècle.

1. The Musée national d'Art moderne is located in the Centre Georges Pompidou. On what floor is the museum?

    _____

2. From what century is the art you find in this museum?

    _____

3. What museum is located at 6, rue de Furstemberg in Paris?

    _____

4. During what hours is this museum open?

    _____

5. Where would you go to see paintings and sculptures by Picasso?

    _____

6. What is the telephone number of this museum?

    _____

7. If you like the sculptures of Rodin, what museum should you visit?

    _____

8. How much in francs is the entrance ticket to this museum and the surrounding park?

    _____

9. What museum is located on the Place de la Concorde in Paris?

    _____

10. From what two centuries is the art you find at the Musée d'Orsay?

    _____

11. If you like the paintings of water lilies by Claude Monet, what museum should you visit?

    _____

12. Which large museum has both temporary and permanent exhibits as well as a restaurant and a café?

    _____

Unit 11

A Match the French expression in column B with its English equivalent in column A.

A		B	
1. hair	_____	a)	le pied
2. nose	_____	b)	l'oreille
3. foot	_____	c)	le genou
4. chest	_____	d)	la tête
5. neck	_____	e)	le nez
6. elbow	_____	f)	la poitrine
7. ear	_____	g)	le cou
8. eye	_____	h)	le coude
9. knee	_____	i)	les cheveux
10. head	_____	j)	l'œil

B Which expression doesn't belong with the others? Circle the letter of the misfit.

1. a) pied   b) Va au tableau.   c) épaule

2. a) menton   b) Écris.   c) main

3. a) Lis.   b) front   c) yeux

4. a) jambe   b) oreille   c) Écoute.

5. a) Parle.   b) doigts de pied   c) bouche

6. a) main   b) Prends une feuille de papier.   c) estomac

C Fill in the missing letters.

1. l'_____eil

2. la den_____

3. le ge_____ou

4. le _____ou

5. la bouc_____e

6. la fig_____re

7. le f_____ont

8. l'_____stomac

9. la jam_____e

10. les cheveu_____

D Answer each question in French.

1. Which part of your body tells you that something is baking in the oven?

    _____

2. What need milk to make them strong?

    _____

3. In order to eat, what do you open?

    _____

4. What bend to help you sit down?

    _____

5. What do you use to throw a ball?

    _____

6. Where would you wear a wedding ring?

    _____

7. Where do women traditionally wear earrings?

    _____

8. Where do women wear lipstick?

    _____

9. Where do you put contact lenses?

    _____

E Complete the sentences with the appropriate body part in French. You will need to know a new word: *entre* (between).

1. Le _____ est entre les cheveux et les yeux.

2. Il y a 32 _____ dans la bouche.

3. La _____ est entre le cou et l'estomac.

4. Tu écoutes le professeur avec les _____ .

5. La _____ est entre le coude et les doigts.

6. Les _____ sont sur la tête.

7. Le _____ est entre les yeux et la bouche.

8. Tu manges avec la _____ et les

    _____ .

9. Le _____ est entre la tête et les épaules.

10. Le _____ est entre le genou et les doigts de pied.

Mots croisés

Vertical

1. «La...fille s'appelle Martine.»
2. «...mère est dans la maison.»
3. Shoulder.
4. «Avec la..., je choisis les réponses applicables.»
5. «Comment vas-...?»
6. «Dis-le...français.»
7. What you comb.
8. «Le...est entre l'épaule et la main.»
10. Where food enters the body.
13. Egg.
15. What pumps the blood.
16. What a shoe covers.
17. «...y a six pièces dans ma maison.»
19. «Les pommes...terre sont délicieuses.»
20. Above your eyebrows.
21. Eye.
22. «Qu'est-ce que c'...?»
23. A dairy product.
24. «Combien font un et six?»
27. What you smell with.

Horizontal

1. Leg.
4. "S'il...plaît."
5. «...parents sont à l'intérieur.»
7. What supports your head.
8. "Un...prix."
9. "Vingt et...."
11. Elbow.
12. Where food is digested.
13. They let you hear.
14. A hot beverage.
16. "Un bon...."
18. You use it to kneel.
20. "Mains..., cœur chaud."
23. They help you speak.
25. The opposite of "non."
26. «Deux...trois font cinq.»
28. What you brush and floss.
29. «...sœur et ton frère sont ici.»

G With your partner play *Jacques dit*, this time with parts of the body. Give your partner a command using a verb and an appropriate part of the body, for example, *Touche le nez*. If you say *Jacques dit* before the command, your partner should perform the action ordered. If you do not say *Jacques dit*, however, your partner should ignore your command. Keep giving orders until your partner either performs incorrectly or makes a motion when you have not said *Jacques dit*. He or she then gives you orders until you make a mistake. Some command forms you might use are *Lève* (Raise), *Baisse* (Lower), *Tourne* (Turn), *Touche* (Touch), *Ouvre* (Open), *Ferme* (Close) and *Couvre* (Cover).

H As you skim various advertisements in French magazines, you will find the names of 12 different parts of the body that you have learned in this lesson. Write the names of these body parts in the spaces that follow the ads.

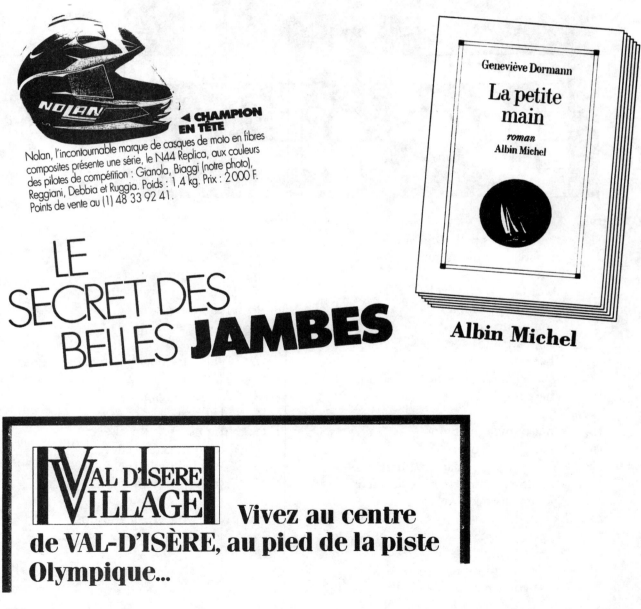

Nom: _____ Date: _____

_____

_____

_____

_____

_____

_____

_____

_____

_____

_____

_____

_____

Unit 12

A Match each French expression in column B with the appropriate description in column A.

A   B

1.   dressy female attire   _____   a)   chemisier
2.   formal male attire   _____   b)   pantoufles
3.   bedtime or casual attire   _____   c)   cravate
4.   worn around the neck   _____   d)   blouson
5.   female attire with a skirt   _____   e)   robe de chambre
6.   footwear with a bathrobe   _____   f)   ceinture
7.   covering for the head   _____   g)   robe
8.   short jacket   _____   h)   manteau
9.   long coat   _____   i)   costume
10. worn to hold up pants   _____   j)   chapeau

B Which article of clothing wouldn't you wear at the same time you wear the other two? Circle the letter of the item that doesn't belong.

1.   a) gants   b) chapeau   c) pyjama

2.   a) chaussures   b) chemisier   c) pantoufles

3.   a) cravate   b) jupe   c) pantalon

4.   a) pantalon   b) chandail   c) costume

5.   a) pantoufles   b) blouson   c) robe de chambre

6.   a) chaussettes   b) robe de laine   c) manteau

C Name the article of clothing in French that you wear or use in the following situations.

1. You wear this over your pajamas. _____

2. You put these on your hands. _____

3. You use this when you blow
   your nose. _____

4. You wear this accessory around
   your waist. _____

5. You wear this on your head. _____

6. You wear these on your feet
   when you go out. _____

D Unscramble the words.

1. napnoalt _____

2. mocesut _____

3. laptefusno _____

4. aumetna _____

5. aymajp _____

6. puje _____

7. sieehcm _____

8. imhcreesi _____

9. tarvace _____

10. msetteenv _____

E Find your way through the clothing store. As you trace your route from the entrance arrow labeled *Entrée* to the exit arrow labeled *Sortie*, list in French the items of clothing you encounter.

_____   _____

_____   _____

_____   _____

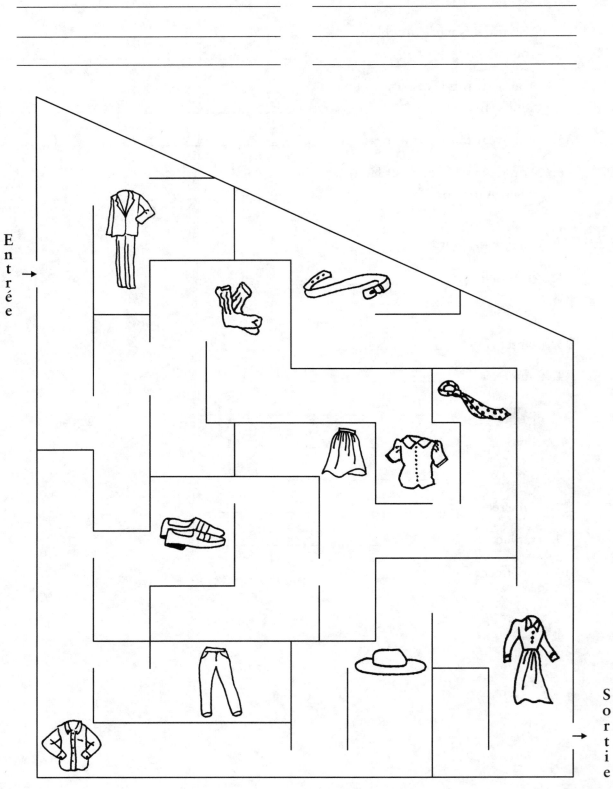

F Circle the following items of clothing in the letter grid. The letters may go forward or backward; they may go up, down, across or diagonally.

1. chemisier
2. cravate
3. costume
4. chemise
5. chaussures
6. chaussettes
7. chandail
8. ceinture
9. chapeau
10. vêtements

11. jupe
12. pantoufles
13. robe de chambre
14. blouson
15. manteau
16. pantalon
17. gants
18. mouchoir
19. pyjama

```
                R E P L C R A V A T E U
                T B I C C O A N P D A E
                U A R H H B Q F S E S J
        E N E D S D R T G I E J S E L F U O T N A P
        T C E I N T U R E T D M E R J C E O I Z A A
        G C H A U S S E T T E S I U O H S A T E D N
        A A H I O U G S U V C E E S A E T N Y A I T
        N C F N O S U O L B H P T S E M A C R P D A
        T Q N U E C H A P E A U T U D I M A E L B L
        S T N E M E T E V O M J L A Z S A Q L U E O
        A R I O H C U O M E B E S H E I J M O V B N
                T A R B J R U M C F E Y
                E M A N T E A U U V R P
                I Y U H M U B Q O N A L
```

G Who wears what and where? Begin by thinking of five names of occupations in French. Say each occupation and your partner will say what someone who has that job typically wears.

EXAMPLE: You say: professeur

Your partner says: costume, chemise, cravate, ceinture, chaussettes, chaussures

Then it's your partner's turn. He or she thinks of five names of places in French. After he or she says each one, you will say what someone in that location typically wears.

EXAMPLE: Your partner says: chambre

You say: robe de chambre, pantoufles

H You're looking for clothing in a French catalogue. Answer the questions about various items.

le chapeau
229f
existe en noir

le pendentif
AGATHA
130f

le pull
149f

la culotte
149f

ELLE ♥

STOP AFFAIRE
E le pyjama
à partir de
85F

G CUIR VÉRITABLE
la ceinture
49f

G La ceinture tressée, en cuir vachette véritable. Boucle à rou-
leau en métal coloris argent. 1 pas-
sant cuir. Larg. 2,5 cm.
1-noir 760.2979   3-marron 750.2133
2-kaki 755.2440   4-marine 750.2109
T. de taille (en cm)
80, 90, 100, 110   **49 F**

H Très agréable à porter, la chemise à rayures en popeline pur
coton. Manches longues. Col à
pointes boutonnées. 1 poche arron-
die. Boutons imitation nacre. Pli mi-
lieu dos. Pans arrondis.
1-bleu 302.9980
2-vert 303.6332
3-bordeaux 303.1870
Encolures (en cm)
37/38, 39/40   **109 F**
41/42, 43/44   **119 F**

H
à partir de
109f
la chemise rayure

7
les bottines
289f

les bottines Naf Naf
7 Sympas et ultra chaudes ! En croûte de
cuir vachette velours, fourrées. Brodées
côtés et soulignées d'un galon fleuri. Lacets
multicolores. Semelle crantée élastomère.
écru 386.7196   noir 390.5691
36, 37, 38, 39, 40, 41   **289 F**
NAF NAF

A
à partir de
219f
existent
doublés

A - LES GANTS en cuir lisse agneau souple

4- la robe 249 F

Le pantalon à partir de **299f**

1. How many different colors does the belt come in?

    _____

2. How much does the dress cost?

    _____

3. What is the brand of the boots?

    _____

4. How much do the men's pants cost?

    _____

5. How much do the men's pajamas cost?

    _____

6. How many different colors does the shirt come in?

    _____

7. How much does the women's hat cost?

    _____

8. How much do the gloves cost?

    _____

9. If you had 500 francs to spend at this store, what items would you buy?

    _____

    _____

Unit 13

A   Write each time using numbers.

1. Il est minuit moins le quart.   _____

2. Il est trois heures et demie.   _____

3. Il est huit heures.   _____

4. Il est cinq heures seize.   _____

5. Il est une heure.   _____

6. Il est onze heures et quart.   _____

7. Il est deux heures moins vingt.   _____

8. Il est midi dix.   _____

B   Answer each question by circling the appropriate response. Watch out for times expressed according to the 24-hour system!

1. At what time does the sun rise?

   a) à six heures dix   b) à dix heures six

2. At what time do you leave for school in the morning?

   a) à quinze heures   b) à sept heures et demie

3. At what time does the Sunday afternoon NFL game start?

   a) à treize heures   b) à neuf heures

4. At what time are you dismissed from school each day?

   a) à quatorze heures et demie   b) à huit heures et demie

5. At what time does the sun set?

   a) à trois heures   b) à dix-neuf heures

6. At what time would you go stargazing?

   a) à six heures   b) à vingt-trois heures

C Answer the following questions giving the times using French words. You will need to know some new words: *prends* (have), *cours* (class).

> EXAMPLE: Tu prends le dîner à quelle heure?
>   <u>À six heures et demie.</u>

1. Tu ouvres les yeux à quelle heure?

   _____

2. Tu prends le petit déjeuner à quelle heure?

   _____

3. Le cours de français commence à quelle heure?

   _____

4. Le cours de français finit à quelle heure?

   _____

5. Tu prends le déjeuner à quelle heure?

   _____

6. Le cours d'anglais est à quelle heure?

   _____

7. Tu dis «Bonne nuit» à quelle heure?

   _____

8. Quelle heure est-il?

   _____

D Identify in French the color generally associated with each item.

1. banane _____

2. chocolat _____

3. océan _____

4. poivre _____

5. lait _____

6. dents _____

7. épinards _____

8. tomates _____

9. café _____

10. pomme _____

11. beurre _____

12. tableau _____

E Each color on the left is a combination of two other colors. Write the French words for the colors that are mixed together.

1. vert = _____ + _____

2. orange = _____ + _____

3. gris = _____ + _____

4. rose = _____ + _____

5. violet = _____ + _____

F Mots croisés

Vertical

1. Color.
2. A seasoning that accompanies pepper.
4. 1:30.
5. «Ma sœur et...enfants sont à la réunion.»
6. Color of grass in the spring.
7. Between your shoulder and your hand.
8. «...quelle couleur est la robe?»
9. «Les robes? ...sont blanches.»
11. "Deux, ..., quatre."
13. «...marraine est-elle ici?»
17. Color of strawberries.
18. «...tard que jamais.»
22. Color of lemons.
24. Color of salt.
26. «...mère s'appelle Laure.»
29. Foot.
31. Color of storm clouds.
34. «Il est dix heures moins...quart.»

Horizontal

3. «... fais-tu?»
5. «André et...femme sont dans le jardin.»
8. The same as 8 down.
10. What time is it?
12. «Il est sept heures...quart.»
14. A warm beverage.
15. Light red.
16. «Il est trois heures moins le....»
19. Color of wood.
20. «Les mouchoirs? ...sont blancs.»
21. «Il est...heure et demie.»
22. «...suis médecin.»
23. "Un, ..., trois."
24. Color of the sky.
25. «Comment vas-...?»
26. When the sun is at its highest point in the sky.
27. «L'habit...fait pas le moine.»
28. «Danielle...au bal avec Bernard.»
30. Color of carrots.
32. Color of pepper.
33. Color resulting from combining red and blue.
35. «Quelle heure...-il?»

G With your partner take turns making quick sketches like the one in the example that show the time. Add a moon or a sun to your drawing to indicate the difference between A.M. and P.M. Ask your partner the time and he or she will answer you based on your sketch.

EXAMPLE:

You show this sketch to your partner and ask: Quelle heure est-il?

Your partner answers: Il est neuf heures.

H Look at the French TV schedule for a Saturday in July. Answer the following questions using information found in the schedule for channels TF1, France 2, France 3, Canal + and M6. You will need to know some new words: *roue* (wheel), *météo* (weather report).

1. At what time and on what channel can you see a rebroadcast of last night's "CBS Evening News"?

   _____

2. At what time can you see "Wheel of Fortune" on TF1?

   _____

3. What American film can you see on Canal + at 11:45 P.M.?

   _____

4. What type of program can you see on TF1 at 8:20 A.M.?

   _____

5. At what time and on what channel can you see a program about animals? What is the program's name?

   _____

6. How many different times during the day can you see a weather report on TF1?

   _____

7. At what time and on what channel can you see "Beverly Hills 90210"?

   _____

8. What is the only channel that doesn't have 24-hour programming?

   _____

TF1

5.05 Histoires naturelles (R)
6.00 Mésaventures
6.30 Club mini - Zig zag
7.20 Club mini
8.20 Télé-shopping
8.50 Club Dorothée vacances
9.30 Le Jacky show maximusic
9.55 Club Dorothée vacances (suite)
10.30 Télévitrine
10.45 Météo des plages
10.50 Ça me dit… et vous ?
11.50 Météo des plages
11.55 La roue de la fortune
12.20 Météo
12.25 Le juste prix
12.50 A vrai dire
12.55 Météo - Trafic infos
13.00 Journal
13.15 Reportages
13.50 Millionnaire
14.10 Ciné gags
14.20 La Une est à vous
14.25 Agence tous risques (R)
15.10 La Une est à vous (suite)
17.40 Ciné gags
17.45 Trente millions d'amis
18.15 Chips (R)
19.05 Beverly Hills
19.55 Loto : premier tirage rouge
20.00 Journal
20.30 Résultats tiercé-quarté+-
quinté+-Météo-Trafic infos
20.35 Loto : deuxième tirage rouge
**20.40 SUCCÈS FOUS DE
L'ÉTÉ (voir ci-contre)**

Patrick Roy fut le roi de
la bonne humeur

22.20 Hoollywood Night
Peter Gunn. Téléfilm américain de
Blake Edwards. Avec Peter Strauss,
Barbara Williams, Jennifer Edwards.
L'histoire. Dans le jardin d'une villa
de Chicago, un homme se fait
électrocuter dans sa piscine. Peter
Gunn, détective privé, se rend dans
son cabaret préféré. Il apprend que
Tony Amatti, un caïd, a envoyé ses
hommes de mains à sa recherche.
Ils le conduisent auprès de Tony qui
l'engage pour retrouver le meurtrier
de Julius Katula, l'homme
électrocuté qui était un chef de la
pègre et surtout son rival…
23.50 Formule foot
0.25 TF1 nuit - Météo
0.30 Histoire des inventions (R)
1.20 TF1 nuit (R)
1.25 L'oreille
3.15 TF1 nuit (R)

3.20 Intrigues (R)
3.45 TF1 nuit (R)
3.55 Passions (R)
4.20 TF1 nuit (R)
4.25 Intrigues
4.50 Musique

France 2

5.00 Et la vie continue
6.05 Cousteau (R)
6.55 Dessin animé
7.00 Debout les petits bouts
8.00 Samedi aventure
10.05 Télévisator 2
12.25 Que le meilleur gagne
13.00 Journal
13.20 Météo
13.25 Rêves d'ailleurs
14.20 Animalia
15.10 Sport passion
16.05 Coupe d'Europe de
gymnastique
17.35 La nuit africaine
19.20 Que le meilleur gagne plus
20.00 Journal
20.40 Journal des courses
20.45 Météo
**20.50 L'ALERTE ROUGE
(voir ci-contre)**
22.20 L'alerte rouge
Le chantier. Téléfilm français de
Gilles Katz. Avec Françoise
Michaud, Bernard-Pierre Donnadieu.
L'histoire. C'est l'été. Les
campings sont pleins. Les touristes
ont envahi les plages. La chaleur et
le vent, propices aux départs de
feux, menacent le départemenr.
Les pompiers sont sur le qui-vive.
Des promoteurs immobiliers
tournent autour du village de
vacances d'Alric, tenu par un
Allemand, kinschoffer, ami de
Jérôme. Une voiture rôde sur les
chemins de montagne…
0.05 Journal de la nuit
0.15 Météo
0.20 Le cercle de minuit
1.20 Fort Boyard (R)
2.50 Les amours des années 50
3.45 Dessin animé
3.50 24 heures d'info
4.05 Les métiers dangereux

France 3

7.00 L'heure du golf
7.30 Bonjour les petits loups
8.15 Les Minikeums
10.05 Continentales d'été
11.00 Top défense
11.30 Mascarines
12.00 12/13
12.05 Estivales
12.45 Journal
13.00 Agatha Christie
14.00 Couleur pays
17.35 Matlock
18.25 Questions pour un champion
18.55 Un livre, un jour
19.00 19/20
19.10 Editions régionales
19.35 19/20 (suite)
19.55 Météo
20.05 Yacapa
20.35 Hugo délire
20.45 LE PIEGE (voir ci-contre)
22.25 Soir 3 - Météo

22.50 Pégase
Anatomie d'une mission orbitale.
La réalité de la vie à bord de la
navette "Atlantis" avec en point de
mire, la volonté de progresser dans
la conquête de l'espace. Autres
sujets : Cap Canaveral, visite du
sanctuaire du port de l'espace.
Championnat d'Europe de vol à
voile 1991. La mission "Antares"
23.40 Les étoiles d'Hollywood
Le film inachevé : I, Claudius.
Avec Charles Laughton, Merle
Oberon, Emlyn Wiliams, Flora
Robson. L'histoire d'un film qui
aurait pu être un chef-d'oeuvre
cinématographique, mais qui n'a
jamais pu voir le jour à l'écran. En
1937, le metteur en scène, Josef
Von Sternberg prépare "I,
Claudius", un film retraçant la vie
d'un empereur romain…

CANAL+

7.00 CBS Evening News. En clair
7.25 Décode pas Bunny
8.20 Scènes de chasse dans le
Ngorongoro (R)
9.05 Sup de fric
Film français de Christian Gion.
Avec Anthony Delon, Cris
Campion, Jean Poiret…
L'histoire. Cyril Dujardin,
directeur d'une école de commerce
pour fils de bonnes familles,
propose à Victor, un petit génie de
l'informatique, de le scolariser
gratuitement. En échange, celui-ci
devra éliminer le virus introduit
dans le système informatique de
l'établissement par un
informaticien licencié…
1re diff. Rediff. : 1, 4, 6, 9, 12/8.
10.35 The Voyager
Rediff. : 2, 7/8.
12.30 Flash infos. En clair
12.35 Farm Aid avec Willie
Nelson. En clair
13.30 Rugby. En différé
15.15 Un innocent sur mesure
16.45 Surprises
17.05 Les superstars du catch
18.05 Canaille peluche
18.30 Batman. En clair
18.55 Fishpolice. En clair
19.15 Canaille peluche. En clair
19.30 Flash infos. En clair
19.35 Le top. En clair
**20.30 L'AFFAIRE KATE
WILLIS (voir ci-contre)**
22.00 Flash infos
22.05 Pétanque : Finale
23.00 Jour de foot
23.45 Ghoulies III
Film américain de John Carl
Buechler. Avec Kevin McCarthy,
Evan MacKenzie, Eva La Rue…
L'histoire. Sur un campus
américain, les Betas et les
Gammas, deux groupes d'étudiants
délurés, se disputent le titre de
"Roi des farceurs". Skip Carter, le
chef des Betas, espère bien
récupérer la couronne. Il se fâche
avec Erin, sa fiancée, qui le
soupçonne de la tromper…
1re diff. Rediff. : 10, 13, 19/8.
1.15 Au pays des Juliets

Dernière diff.
2.50 Cabo Blanco
Rediff. : 3, 5/8.
4.20 Vengeance diabolique
Dernière diff.
6.00 Sans oublier les enfants (R)

M6

5.10 La prochaine escale (R)
6.00 Culture pub
6.30 Boulevard des clips
8.30 M6 Kid
10.05 M6 boutique
10.35 Flash-info-conso
10.40 Multitop
12.00 Mariés deux enfants
12.25 Ma sorcière bien-aimée (R)
12.55 Equalizer
13.50 Supercopter
14.45 Département S
15.40 Amicalement vôtre
16.35 Flashback
17.00 Culture rock
17.30 Le Saint
18.25 Turbo
19.00 Drôles de dames
19.54 6 Minutes - Météo
20.00 Loin de ce monde
20.35 Tranche de rire
20.45 La saga du samedi
**20.50 LES DISPARUES
D'EDIMBOURG (voir ci-contre)**
23.10 Officier et top-model
Téléfilm américain de Reza
Badiyi. Avec Melody Anderson,
Ed Marinaro, Greg Monoghan…
L'histoire. L'officier de police,
Jennifer Oaks, dit Jen, est en
patrouille avec Chris, son
coéquipier. Ce dernier lui annonce
qu'il veut changer d'équipier car
sa future épouse n'apprécie pas
qu'il travaille avec une femme. Jen
fait, désormais, équipe avec Bill,
qui l'invite à dîner…
0.45 6 minutes
0.55 Boulevard des clips
1.20 Nouba
1.45 Les enquêtes de Capital (R)
2.10 Les lumières dans la ville (R)
3.05 Culture rock
3.30 Les défis de l'océan (R)
4.25 Culture pub
4.50 Renouveau de la préhistoire
française (R)

Unit 14

A Complete the name of each musical work.

1. *Daphnis* _____

2. *Pieces* _____

3. *The Spanish* _____

4. *Castor* _____

5. *The* _____

B Answer each question by circling the correct letter.

1. Who won the Prix de Rome award?

    a) Bizet   b) Rameau   c) Ravel

2. Who was considered to be the master of harmony?

    a) Ravel   b) Bizet   c) Rameau

3. Who was a composer of the Baroque period?

    a) Ravel   b) Rameau   c) Bizet

4. Who used musical sounds to create certain impressions?

    a) Rameau   b) Bizet   c) Ravel

5. Who studied at the Paris Conservatory of Music?

    a) Bizet   b) Ravel   c) Rameau

6. Who wrote *Pieces for the Harpsichord*?

    a) Rameau   b) Bizet   c) Ravel

7. Who died without much recognition for his masterpiece?

    a) Bizet   b) Rameau   c) Ravel

8. Who wrote vocal music as well as ballets and pieces for the orchestra?

    a) Rameau   b) Ravel   c) Bizet

C Write the name of the musician who fits each description.

1. He used folk music to form the basis for his compositions.

   _____

2. He began his musical career at the age of six.

   _____

3. He played the organ and the harpsichord.

   _____

4. He wrote musical compositions for large orchestras.

   _____

5. He died at an early age.

   _____

6. He wrote the opera *Carmen*.

   _____

7. His musical achievements were highly regarded during his lifetime.

   _____

8. He lived during the eighteenth century.

   _____

D Unscramble the words. They are either names of the musicians or English names of musical instruments mentioned in this unit.

1. tibez   _____

2. narog   _____

3. earmua   _____

4. laver   _____

5. cirshodraph   _____

6. onipa   _____

E Match the French name of the musical instrument in column B with its corresponding description in column A.

A		B
1. You traditionally hear this during religious services.	_____	a) la clarinette
2. This instrument is like a long tube and has a high-pitched sound.	_____	b) le violon
		c) la trompette
3. You beat this with sticks.	_____	d) l'orgue
4. This woodwind instrument needs a reed.	_____	e) la batterie
5. You play this with a bow.	_____	f) la flûte
6. This instrument plays reveille, a military wake up call.	_____	g) la guitare
7. Country singers often play this.	_____	

F   Circle the following words, names and expressions in the letter grid. The letters may go forward or backward; they may go up, down, across or diagonally.

1. *Pieces for the Harpsichord*
2. *Castor and Pollux*
3. *Carmen*
4. ballet
5. opera
6. Ravel
7. *The Spanish Hour*
8. *Daphnis and Chloé*
9. Bizet
10. *The Waltz*
11. conservatory
12. Rameau
13. Paris
14. Dijon
15. Baroque
16. Prix de Rome
17. impressions
18. organ
19. musical
20. theorist
21. composer
22. Ciboure
23. folk music
24. orchestra
25. piano
26. harmony
27. masterpiece
28. works
29. sounds
30. France

```
            A S L E M V O A L E S F
            W K M T I E T R R D R H
          E R I N E R U O H H S I N A P S E H T H
          Z C O M P O S E R E O U N T P M A A R E
O O T O R G A N H W I X R L O C E L P O D B A L L E T S
S E U N S I O S T Z C P L S E R N H E I Y S R N I E E H
M P T H E W A L T Z A E D B A B I O T N A P E A U H Z E
C A R T S E H C R O L D P O A T L S J E S N P Q S O I R
L S P I E C E S F O R T H E H A R P S I C H O R D N B T
A C D M I A B U A E M A R R A G A H T A D R C R U O P V
C I B O U R E H A R M O N Y R E V R O N A P I E R E M A
S C I S U M K L O F M S U D I A E C L B S R E S C I S O
K U O N J E M O R E D X I R P U L S N O I S S E R P M I
W S I R O N C O N S E R V A T O R Y P F I C O E R E Y R
          D A P H N I S A N D C H L O E H S N H T
          E C E I P R E T S A M I S L A R P O T L
            D A T H E O R I S T U S
            R P O C C H I M B A O X
```

G Interview your partner about his or her musical tastes. Ask your partner the following questions and note his or her answers.

1. What is your favorite type of music?

    _____

2. Who are your favorite male and female singers?

    _____

3. Who is your favorite group?

    _____

4. Can you name a singer or group from outside the U.S.?

    _____

5. Have you ever seen any singers or groups in concert? If so, which singer(s) or group(s)?

    _____

    _____

6. Do you play any musical instruments? If so, which one(s)?

    _____

    _____

Then reverse roles so that your partner interviews you.

H In Paris there are many concerts each day for music lovers with a wide range of tastes—classical, blues, jazz, rock, reggae, etc. Look at these descriptions of various types of concerts and answer the questions that follow. You will need to know some new words: *places* (seats), *église* (church).

Sainte-Chapelle. — 21h00 Ensemble d'archets européen Carl Brainich. « Carmen », de Bizet (extraits), « Les quatre saisons », de Vivaldi, « Divertimento K 138 », de Mozart.

FESTIVAL MUSIQUE EN L'ILE
EGLISE SAINT LOUIS EN L'ILE
Mercredi 28 juillet & samedi 31 à 20h45 &
Dimanche 1er août à 17h
BACH Concertos pour Violon
Cantate "Ich habe genug"
Ens. Inst. Ste Geneviève - D. Valgalier, violon

«**LADY SINGS THE JAZZ**»
Josiane Saint-Louis
21 H. LE NOUVEAU CAFE
13-15, rue du Maine - 75014 Paris
Tél. : 43.21.65.29
BAR : 80 F - RESTAURANT : 150 F
SPECTACLE COMPRIS

Sainte-Chapelle. — 21h00 Concertsolo. Festival Musique en l'Ile. Gabriel FUMET, flûte. Oeuvres de Bach, Telemann, Mozart, Paganini, Debussy. Loc. 40 30 10 13. Pl. 120/100/75F.

GAMBRINUS, 62, rue des Lombards (M° Châtelet). 42.21.10.30. Tous les soirs : **Bar à ambiance Rock et Country**, de 22h à 5h du matin.

Eglise de la Madeleine
mardi 10 août à 21 h
REQUIEM de MOZART
Chœur et Orchestre: Le Sinfonietta de Paris
FNAC - VIRGIN

1. If you go to the Sainte-Chapelle, you can hear the opera *Carmen*. Who is the French composer of this opera?

   _____

2. At the same concert you will hear music by two other famous composers. Who are they?

   _____

3. What time does this concert begin?

   _____

4. Gabriel Fumet is also giving a concert at the Sainte-Chapelle. What instrument does he play?

   _____

5. How much do the seats cost for this concert?

   _____

6. Where can you go to hear Mozart's *Requiem*?

   _____

7. What instrument is featured in the Bach concertos?

   _____

8. If you go to a club called Gambrinus, what kind of music will you hear?

   _____

9. Until what time is this club open?

   _____

10. What is the name of the jazz singer at Le Nouveau Café?

   _____

Unit 15

A Match each French expression in column B with its English equivalent in column A.

A		B	
1. sun	_____	a)	froid
2. weather	_____	b)	temps
3. summer	_____	c)	frais
4. season	_____	d)	soleil
5. cold	_____	e)	Il pleut.
6. It's snowing.	_____	f)	printemps
7. wind	_____	g)	vent
8. spring	_____	h)	Il neige.
9. It's raining.	_____	i)	été
10. cool	_____	j)	saison

B You have been selected to go to France for a year as an exchange student. You have written a packing list. Explain in French why you're taking the following items.

1. warm clothing

   En hiver à Reims il fait _____ .

2. lightweight clothing

   Au printemps à Bordeaux il fait _____ .

3. coat and hat

   En automne à Strasbourg il fait _____ et il fait du

   _____ .

4. umbrella

   Au printemps à Paris il _____ .

5. swimsuit

   En été à Biarritz il fait _____ .

6. ski suit

   En hiver dans les Alpes il _____ .

7. shorts and T-shirts

   En été dans les Pyrénées il fait _____ .

8. sunscreen

   En été à Marseille il fait du _____ .

9. mittens or gloves

   En hiver à Lille il fait _____ .

10. raincoat

   En automne à Rouen le temps est _____ .

C Write a sentence in French that describes the weather associated with each of the following items.

1. clouds _____

2. toboggan _____

3. windshield wipers _____

4. snowsuit _____

5. rake _____

6. perspiration _____

7. atmospheric electricity _____

8. noise in the sky _____

9. sunglasses _____

D Name the season in French when the following events usually take place.

1. Some birds fly south. _____

2. Some animals hibernate. _____

3. It feels better to be in the shade than in the sun. _____

4. The air gets warmer and the snow starts to melt. _____

5. You carve pumpkins. _____

6. Trees begin to bud. _____

E Name the season in French when the following weather is typical.

1. Il fait chaud. _____

2. Il fait du vent et il pleut. _____

3. Il neige. _____

4. Il fait du vent et il fait frais. _____

5. Il fait humide. _____

6. Il fait très froid. _____

F Find your way through the maze. As you trace your route beginning at the entrance arrow, use the picture clue to write a sentence in French describing each weather condition you encounter.

_____   _____

_____   _____

_____   _____

_____   _____

_____   _____

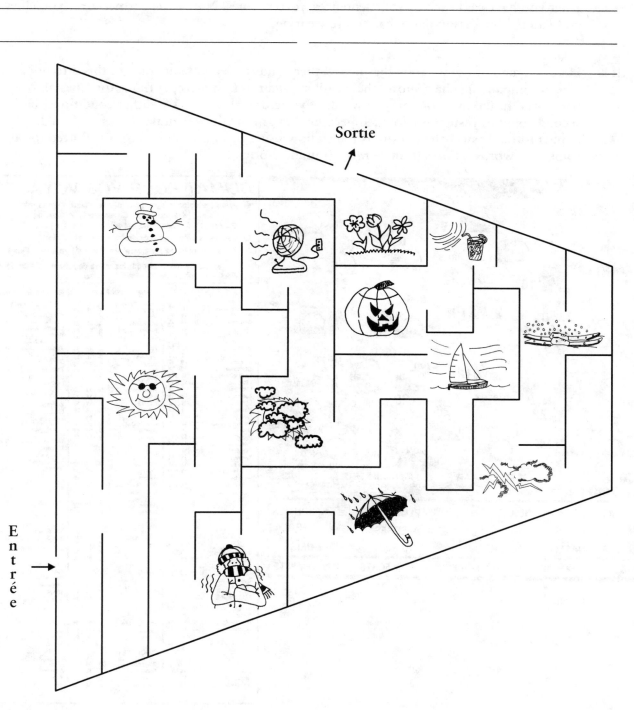

G Make a list of as many French sentences as you can that describe the weather. Say each sentence as a clue for your partner. He or she will say the name of the appropriate season in French and also will say, if possible, what he or she is wearing.

> EXAMPLE: You say: Il neige.
> Your partner says: C'est l'hiver.
> Je porte un manteau et des gants.

After you have said each of your sentences, reverse roles. Now your partner gives you clues and you tell the season and what you're wearing.

H Here is a map of France showing the weather conditions and temperatures this afternoon. The accompanying chart shows the weather conditions and temperatures for cities all over the world. In the first column you will find yesterday afternoon's weather conditions; in the second column, yesterday's low temperature; and in the third column, yesterday's high temperature. Answer the questions that follow using this information. You will need to know some new words: *pluies* (rain), *orages* (thunderstorms).

METEO FRANCE

Lille 19
Brest 17
Paris 20
20
21
18
20
19
Dijon 19
18 Nantes
18 Lyon
22
Bordeaux 22
20
23 26
Toulouse 25 25 25 25
Marseille
Nice 25

AUJOURD'HUI A 14 HEURES

○ CIEL CLAIR A PEU NUAGEUX ||||||| PLUIES   ≈ BRUMES
◑ VARIABLE   ::::::: AVERSES   ≋ VERGLAS
▬ TRES NUAGEUX A COUVERT   ⚡ ORAGES   ❄ NEIGE

VENTS   → FAIBLES   ⇒ MODERES   ⇛ FORTS   ⇛ TEMPETE

CLIMAT POUR VOS VOYAGES

- **Première colonne : temps d'hier en début d'après midi.**
  (S : soleil ; N : nuageux ; C : couvert ; P : pluie ; A : averse ; O : orage ; B : brume ou brouillard ; * : neige.)
- **Deuxième colonne : température matinale d'hier.**
- **Troisième colonne : température d'hier (1) en début d'après-midi.**

(1) Ou d'avant-hier pour les villes des États-Unis de des pays d'Asie en raison des fuseaux horaires.

FRANCE			
Ajaccio	N	20	22
Biarritz	N	14	19
Bordeaux	N	13	20
Brest	N	11	17
Cherbourg	N	11	17
Clermont-F	A	13	16
Dijon	N	11	14
Dinard	N	11	15
Embrun	N	9	17
Grenoble	N	10	16
La Rochelle	N	15	18
Lille	N	12	15
Limoges	N	9	14
Lorient	N	13	16
Lyon	N	11	16
Marseille	N	15	22
Nancy	N	11	17
Nantes	N	12	18
Nice	N	18	24
Paris	N	12	15
Pau	N	13	18
Perpignan	N	17	23
Rennes	N	11	18
Rouen	N	11	17
St-Étienne	A	10	12
Strasbourg	N	11	16
Toulouse	N	13	19
Tours	N	10	17

ESPAGNE - PORTUGAL			
Barcelone	N	18	22
Las Palmas	S	19	23
Madrid	S	14	26
Marbella	S	22	26
Palma de Maj.	S	17	26
Séville	S	19	33
Lisbonne	S	16	27
Madère	S	19	22
Porto	S	13	22

ITALIE			
Florence	C	19	17
Milan	N	15	24
Naples	N	18	25
Olbia	N	18	26
Palerme	S	24	26
Reggio Cal.	N	25	26
Rimini	C	20	17
Rome	S	17	25

GRÈCE - TURQUIE			
Athènes	S	27	32
Corfou	S	22	27
Patras	S	23	29
Rhodes	S	27	30
Salonique	S	23	28
Ankara	S	19	29
Istanbul	S	21	27

EUROPE

ILES BRITANNIQUES			
Brighton	N	11	16
Edimbourg	N	8	15
Londres	C	10	17
Cork	C	10	15
Dublin	N	8	15

ALLEMAGNE - AUTRICHE			
Berlin	N	12	17
Bonn	A	10	14
Hambourg	C	12	16
Munich	N	10	14
Vienne	N	14	19

BENELUX			
Luxembourg	N	10	14
Bruxelles	S	12	15
Amsterdam	A	12	13

PAYS NORDIQUES			
Copenhague	P	12	12
Helsinki	S	19	23
Oslo	P	10	13
Stockholm	C	21	18

SUISSE			
Bâle	A	11	13
Berne	A	10	11
Genève	A	11	14

C.E.I.			
St-Petersbrg	N	21	23
Moscou	N	16	19
Odessa	N	19	21

EUROPE CENTRALE			
Belgrade	N	14	17
Budapest	S	13	22
Prague	O	10	11
Varsovie	N	11	15

RESTE DU MONDE

AFRIQUE DU NORD			
Agadir	S	18	30
Alger	S	19	28
Casablanca	S	18	25
Djerba	S	24	28
Marrakech	S	18	30
Tunis	S	22	29

AFRIQUE			
Abidjan	C	24	28
Dakar	N	26	28
Le Cap	P	11	14

PROCHE-ORIENT			
Beyrouth	S	27	30
Eilat	–	–	–
Le Caire	S	23	33

ÉTATS-UNIS - CANADA			
Boston	S	25	32
Chicago	C	19	25
Houston	S	28	30
Los Angeles	S	19	22
Miami	O	25	29
New York	S	29	32
Nouv.-Orléans	C	24	29
San Francisco	S	13	19
Montréal	S	20	29

CARAIBES			
Ft-d.-France	N	26	30
Pte-à-Pitre	–	–	–
San Juan	O	27	23

EXTRÊME-ORIENT			
Bangkok	N	28	34
Hongkong	N	27	31
Pékin	P	27	27
Saigon	–	–	–
Singapour	C	29	30
Tokyo	C	22	25

AMÉR. CENTR. ET SUD			
Acapulco	S	25	34
Buenos Aires	S	3	11
Cancun	N	23	33
Lima	C	17	19
Mexico	S	13	24
Rio de Jan.	C	19	24
Santiago	S	-4	11

PACIFIQUE			
Aukland	B	5	7
Papeete	S	24	29
Sydney	N	13	16

1. What is today's temperature in Paris?

   _____

2. Is this higher or lower than yesterday's high temperature in Paris?

   _____

3. Around what city is it raining this afternoon?

   _____

4. Where in France is it snowing today?

   _____

5. In which two cities is the sky clear this afternoon?

   _____

6. What city in France had the highest temperature yesterday?

   _____

7. In what French cities did the sun shine yesterday?

   _____

8. Was it warmer yesterday in Rome or in Buenos Aires?

   _____

9. What city in the U.S. had thunderstorms yesterday?

   _____

10. According to yesterday's weather conditions and temperatures, would you have preferred to be in New York or in Paris? Why?

   _____

   _____

Unit 16

A Match the French expression in column B with its English equivalent in column A.

	A			B	
1.	birthday	_____	a)	jour	
2.	today	_____	b)	hier	
3.	week	_____	c)	demain	
4.	day	_____	d)	semaine	
5.	month	_____	e)	anniversaire	
6.	holiday	_____	f)	fête	
7.	tomorrow	_____	g)	mois	
8.	yesterday	_____	h)	aujourd'hui	

B Circle the letter of the correct answer to each question.

1. Quel est le jour après mercredi?

   a) mardi   b) samedi   c) jeudi

2. Quel est le jour avant lundi?

   a) dimanche   b) vendredi   c) mardi

3. Quel est le mois après décembre?

   a) juin   b) novembre   c) janvier

4. Quel est le mois avant avril?

   a) mai   b) mars   c) juillet

5. Quel est le jour après aujourd'hui?

   a) demain   b) hier   c) anniversaire

6. Quel est le jour avant aujourd'hui?

   a) mois   b) hier   c) demain

7. Il y a combien de jours en mai?

   a) 25   b) 31   c) 5

8. Il y a combien de jours de classe dans une semaine?

   a) 7   b) 5   c) 31

C Write the days of the week in order beginning with the French word for Monday.

1. _____

2. _____

3. _____

4. _____

5. _____

6. _____

7. _____

D Write these dates in French. Follow the model.

      EXAMPLE: Thursday, February 28
                   <u>jeudi, le vingt-huit février</u>

1. Saturday, June 1

    _____

2. Wednesday, April 13

    _____

3. Sunday, July 19

    _____

4. Friday, May 21

    _____

5. Tuesday, August 12

    _____

6. Monday, January 16

    _____

E Unscramble the words.

1. rimda   _____

2. devinrde   _____

3. rotboec   _____

4. roju   _____

5. teluijl   _____

6. reevfir   _____

7. drecemir   _____

8. osim   _____

9. tade   _____

10. nameise   _____

F Express the year in French. Follow the model.

EXAMPLE: 1988

mil neuf cent quatre-vingt-huit

1. 1945

_____

2. 1776

_____

3. 1995

_____

4. 1492

_____

5. 1918

_____

6. The year you were born.

_____

G With your classmates play "Birthday Lineup" in French. In this game all students will line up in the chronological order of their dates of birth. Begin by asking one classmate his or her birthday.

EXAMPLE: You say: Quelle est la date de ton anniversaire?
          Your partner says: La date de mon anniversaire est le onze juin.

Then depending on when your birthday is, arrange yourself to the right or left of this person. You will need to ask as many classmates as possible their dates of birth in order to know if you should stand in line to the right or left of them. At the end when everyone is lined up in the correct birth order, each of you will say in turn your date of birth so that the entire class can check the accuracy of the lineup.

H Imagine that you are a tourist in Paris. Besides seeing the city's highlights, you also want to visit some of the famous sites in the surrounding area. Look at the schedule of tours offered by Cityrama and answer the questions that follow. You will need to know some new words: *grandes eaux* (fountains), *château* (castle).

			Pages	Lundi	Mardi	Mercredi	Jeudi	Vendredi	Samedi	Dimanche
VISITES DES ENVIRONS DE PARIS	VO	VERSAILLES ORIENTATION	16 / 17		●	●	●	●	●	●
	VA	VERSAILLES APPARTEMENTS	17		●	●	●	●		●
	VS	VERSAILLES GRANDES EAUX	18			●		●	●	
	F	FONTAINEBLEAU ET BARBIZON	18	●			●		●	
	FO	FONTAINEBLEAU ORIENTATION	18			●				●
	CH	CHARTRES	19		●		●			
	CY	CHANTILLY (Château de Chantilly)	19		●		●		●	
	G	GIVERNY (Maison de Monet)	20		●				●	
	VT	VERSAILLES ET TRIANONS	20			●		●	●	
	VC	VERSAILLES APPARTEMENTS + CHARTRES	20						●	
	VF	VERSAILLES APPARTEMENTS + FONTAINEBLEAU-BARBIZON	20				●		●	
	FV	FONTAINEBLEAU ET VAUX-LE-VICOMTE	21						●	●
	MG	MONET ET LES AMÉRICAINS A GIVERNY	21			●	●	●	●	●
	AG	AUVERS S/OISE ET GIVERNY	23	●					●	
	ED	EURO DISNEYLAND®	24			●				
PROVINCES	RC	REIMS CHAMPAGNE								

1. On which days can you take a tour to Euro Disneyland?

_____

2. Which is the only day the Fontainebleau orientation tour is offered?

_____

3. If you like paintings by the French Impressionist Monet, when can you go to Giverny to see his house?

_____

4. Which is the only day you can go to Versailles and see the fountains in action?

   _____

5. On which days can you combine trips to Chartres and Versailles?

   _____

6. Which days can you choose from if you want to see Versailles and Fontainebleau on the same tour?

   _____

7. Which is the only day that you can take a tour of the castle at Chantilly?

   _____

8. By looking at this schedule, you can tell that many of the national monuments, castles, museums, etc. in France are closed one day a week. On which day?

   _____

Unit 17

A Match the authors in column B with the appropriate expressions in column A.

A		B
1. romanticism	_____	a) Pierre Corneille
2. symbolism	_____	b) Victor Hugo
3. classicism	_____	c) Charles Baudelaire
4. 1821-67	_____	
5. 1802-85	_____	
6. 1606-84	_____	
7. studied Latin and Greek	_____	
8. was interested in politics	_____	
9. practiced law	_____	
10. wanted to help the less fortunate	_____	
11. translated Poe's poems into French	_____	
12. exiled by the French government	_____	

B Match the literary movements in column B with their corresponding characteristics in column A.

A

1. objects that represent qualities _____

2. lofty ideals (duty, patriotism, _____
   courage)

3. strong feelings _____

4. the 1600s _____

5. the 1800s _____

6. the artist Delacroix _____

7. concern for oppressed people _____

8. experimentation with words _____

B

a) symbolism

b) romanticism

c) classicism

C Complete the sentences by adding the missing words. They may be types of literary works, titles of literary works or names of authors.

1. *Mélite* is a _____ by Pierre Corneille.

2. *Les _____ du mal* is a collection of poetry by Charles Baudelaire.

3. *Les Misérables* is a novel by _____ .

4. *Le Cid* is a play by _____ .

5. *Les Feuilles d'* _____ is a collection of poetry by Victor Hugo.

6. *Hernani* is a play by _____ .

D Write the name of the author that fits each description.

1. He became famous for his word pictures.

    _____

2. The principal character in his masterpiece is a Spanish hero.

    _____

3. He is considered to be the best writer of the romantic period in France.

    _____

4. The end of his short life was marked by poverty and ill health.

    _____

5. He sympathized with people who were treated unjustly.

    _____

6. He wrote poetry, novels and plays.

    _____

7. Many of his plays are about Greek and Roman heroes.

    _____

8. He was born in Paris.

    _____

E Unscramble the words. They are either names of the authors or English names of the types of literary works that these authors wrote.

1. madar   _____

2. railabedue   _____

3. licerenol   _____

4. epyort   _____

5. ough   _____

6. losevn   _____

F   Mots croisés

Vertical

1. Corneille is considered to be the father of...drama.
2. ...is the masterpiece of Corneille.
3. «Ma mère s'appelle Hélène,...mon père s'appelle Charles.»
4. «Quel jour est-...?»
5. Corneille was born in....
6. «J'...faim.»
8. «Tout est bien...bien.»
9. Baudelaire was a....
12. Corneille's first play.
13. *Les*...is a novel by Hugo that became a Broadway musical.
14. Baudelaire translated the poems written by....
15. Hugo is considered to be the best writer of the...period.
24. ...cared about the less fortunate.
26. Corneille studied....
27. A wilting flower might represent....
29. The Mediterranean Sea is "la...Méditerranée."
30. "Comme..., comme ça."

Horizontal

1. ...was a classical dramatist.
5. Corneille wrote about Greek and...heroes.
7. In *Le Cid* the main character is a national....
10. «...habites-tu?»
11. Using a flower to represent beauty is an example of....
14. Corneille's first name.
16. «Quelle heure est-...?»
17. «Les quatre saisons sont l'automne, l'hiver, le printemps et....»
18. «Il neige...hiver.»
19. Corneille studied Latin and....
20. Baudelaire liked poetry and....
21. ...is a play by Hugo.
22. All's well that...well.
23. "Comme ci, comme...."
25. ...was a symbolist poet.
28. *Les Fleurs*...is a collection of poetry.
30. Same as 30 down.
31. Baudelaire was born in....
32. Hugo was sent into...by the French government.

G What kind of books do you like to read? Decide if you prefer mysteries, adventure stories, science fiction or romance novels. Your teacher will designate each corner of your classroom as one of these four kinds of books. Go to the corner that represents your favorite. Pair up with a partner. Each of you tells the other why you like these books, the last book of this kind you read, its author and something about the plot. Then get together with another pair of students in your corner so that you can tell the new pair what your partner has told you. Finally, a spokesperson from each of the four groups tells the entire class something about what students from that group like to read.

H Imagine that you are looking for a good novel to read in French. You consult the weekly list of the 12 best-sellers to see what is available. Answer the questions that follow. You will need to know some new words: *classement précédent* (previous ranking), *éditeurs* (publishers).

LIVRES EN TÊTE

ROMANS

TITRES	AUTEURS	EDITEURS	CLASSEMENT PRÉCÉDENT	NOMBRES DE SEMAINES
1 SOTOS	Philippe Djian	Gallimard	1	4
2 L'ENFANT-ROI	Robert Merle	de Fallois	2	10
3 LES RÊVES DES AUTRES	John Irving	Seuil	10	3
4 L'ENFANT DES SEPT MERS	Paul-Loup Sulitzer	Stock	3	7
5 VU DE L'EXTÉRIEUR	Katherine Pancol	Seuil	7	2
6 JESSIE	Stephen King	Albin Michel	6	5
7 LE DIEU DES PAPILLONS	Jacques Lanzmann	Lattès	-	2
8 BLANCHE	Arlette Cousture	La Table ronde	5	5
9 L'AME DE LA VALLÉE	Christian Signol	Laffont	-	-
10 QUINZE ANS	Philippe Labro	Gallimard	9	19
11 JOURNAL DU DEHORS	Annie Ernaux	Gallimard	4	4
12 LA BOUBOULINA	Michel de Grèce	Plon	-	-

1. What is the name of this week's best-selling novel? Who is the author?

   _____

   _____

2. What was this novel's ranking last week? How many weeks has it been on the list?

   _____

   _____

3. Which novel has been on the list for the longest time? How long?

_____

_____

4. Which novels are on the list for the first time this week?

_____

5. What publisher has published three of these best-sellers?

_____

6. How many of the best-selling authors are female?

_____

7. Which two books were ranked higher this week than they were last week?

_____

8. What two American authors do you recognize on this list?

_____

Unit 18

A Match each English expression in column B with its French equivalent in column A.

A			B	
1.	vélo	_____	a)	to dance
2.	match	_____	b)	beach
3.	cheval	_____	c)	picnic
4.	boum	_____	d)	bike
5.	danser	_____	e)	to read
6.	plage	_____	f)	museum
7.	lire	_____	g)	party
8.	nager	_____	h)	game
9.	pique-nique	_____	i)	horse
10.	musée	_____	j)	to swim

B Which expression is the most appropriate answer to the question? Circle the letter of the best answer.

1. Tu vas à la boum ce soir?

   a) Oui. Il y a de la musique.

   b) Où vas-tu ce soir?

   c) Pourquoi?

2. Tu veux m'accompagner?

   a) Pour voir le festival Delacroix.

   b) Le Louvre est un musée.

   c) Où ça?

3. Où vas-tu ce soir?

   a) Moi aussi!

   b) Je vais à la boum.

   c) Bien sûr.

4. Où est le pique-nique?

   a) Au Louvre.

   b) À la plage.

   c) J'aime faire du cheval.

5. Qu'est-ce que tu aimes faire?

   a) Bien sûr.

   b) Où ça?

   c) J'adore faire du ski.

6. Où vas-tu aujourd'hui?

   a) Diversité réjouit.

   b) J'adore lire.

   c) Au match de football.

7. Quels sports fais-tu?

   a) Je vais à la boum.

   b) Demain il y a un pique-nique.

   c) J'aime nager.

C Complete each sentence with a word from the box.

soir   **nager**   *fais*   sûr   **veux**
Louvre   basket-ball   adore

1. Je fais du _____ .

2. J'aime _____ .

3. Où vas-tu ce _____ ?

4. Bien _____ .

5. Je vais au _____ .

6. Tu _____ m'accompagner?

7. Quels sports _____ -tu?

8. J'_____ faire du ski.

D Tell what sport you are playing if you hear the following expressions.

    EXAMPLE: free kick, goal, pass
    <u>Je fais du football.</u>

1. strike, stolen base, out

    _____

2. spike, serve, net ball

    _____

3. love, deuce, serve

    _____

4. free throw, slam dunk, foul

    _____

5. throw-in, penalty kick, heading

    _____

E Unscramble the words.

1. legap   _____

2. nue-qiepuqi   _____

3. ubmo   _____

4. labotlof   _____

5. smeue   _____

6. belly-loval   _____

7. suumeqi   _____

8. thacm   _____

F Interview five of your classmates to find out what they like to do in their free time. Ask each student the questions that follow and record each answer (*oui* or *non*) in the space provided on this sheet.

	Student 1	Student 2	Student 3	Student 4	Student 5
1. Tu aimes nager?	_____	_____	_____	_____	_____
2. Tu aimes danser?	_____	_____	_____	_____	_____
3. Tu aimes les boums?	_____	_____	_____	_____	_____
4. Tu aimes faire du volley-ball?	_____	_____	_____	_____	_____
5. Tu aimes faire du tennis?	_____	_____	_____	_____	_____
6. Tu aimes faire du basket-ball?	_____	_____	_____	_____	_____
7. Tu aimes faire du ski?	_____	_____	_____	_____	_____
8. Tu aimes faire du vélo?	_____	_____	_____	_____	_____

G Imagine that you are going to spend a weekend in the French region about an hour west of Paris called Perche. This part of France is a wooded rural area known for its large horses, called Percherons. Answer the questions that follow about what things you can do here based on the map from the local tourist bureau. A new expression you will need to know is *syndicat d'initiative* (tourist bureau).

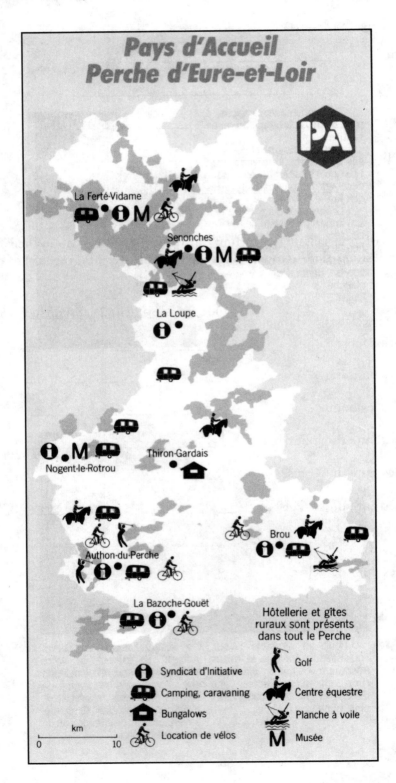

1. Of the eight towns shown, how many have tourist bureaus?

   _____

2. If you want to go windsurfing, what two towns could you choose to stay in?

   _____

3. What town offers bungalows?

   _____

4. What towns have facilities for camping?

   _____

5. Where would you stay if you were interested in playing golf?

   _____

6. In what town can you rent a bicycle and also visit a museum?

   _____

7. In what three areas is horseback riding not available?

   _____

8. Are there more things to do in the central or southern part of Perche?

   _____

9. Which town in Perche would you choose to stay in? Why?

   _____

   _____

H Circle the following words, names and expressions in the letter grid. The letters may go forward or backward; they may go up, down, across or diagonally.

1. ce soir
2. pique-nique
3. Delacroix
4. boum
5. faire du cheval
6. basket-ball
7. match
8. Louvre
9. musique
10. accompagner
11. danser
12. vélo
13. pourquoi
14. festival
15. bien sûr

16. tennis
17. nager
18. plage
19. j'adore
20. musée
21. diversité
22. sports
23. volley-ball
24. lire
25. qu'est-ce que
26. ski
27. tu veux
28. il y a
29. n'est-ce pas
30. football

```
        O P N A T E E N D D Q L
        L I S A P E C T S E N L
        E I F O O T B A L L J A
    E D M I V R A K I D M I L A C B E B L N
    P I Q U E N I Q U E O S D C E T E I A O
    N V L S T T R L E U I O O R U E S E V N
    T E D Y E D E E Q S R M M O Q K U N I O
    E R A N A E D R N E P B C I I S M S T S
    A S N S I V U E G A L P O X S A L U S C
    M I S S S O C I G A B M I U U B V R E T
    S T E T P O H N A U H C T A M E Q S F E
    R E R N O E E U Q E C T S E U Q O P D V
        R R V L O U V R E X V I
        T N A G E R D N L E R U
        S L L A B Y E L L O V E
```

Unit 19

A Match each French expression in column B with its corresponding description in column A.

A

1. The person who helps you in a store. _____
2. What you say when you don't need the salesclerk's help. _____
3. A kind of fruit. _____
4. A shopping center. _____
5. The opposite of "cheap." _____
6. What you say to ask the price of something. _____
7. A sign that indicates a price reduction. _____
8. The coins the cashier gives you back. _____

B

a) C'est combien?
b) cher
c) centre commercial
d) vendeur
e) monnaie
f) Je regarde seulement.
g) pêche
h) soldes

B Which item in each group costs the most? Circle the letter of the item that generally is the most expensive.

1. a) une règle   b) trois pêches   c) un manteau
2. a) un CD   b) un verre de lait   c) deux œufs
3. a) un mouchoir   b) une chaise   c) cinq tomates
4. a) un crayon   b) une chemise   c) un vélo
5. a) des baskets   b) une tasse de café   c) une corbeille à papier
6. a) une maison   b) une ceinture   c) un jus de fruit

C Which expression is the most appropriate answer to the question? Circle the letter of the best answer.

1. Ce sandwich, c'est combien?

   a) Quelque chose d'autre?

   b) Ça coûte 15,00 francs.

   c) Mais non, je regarde seulement.

2. Qu'est-ce que tu vas acheter?

   a) Des fruits.

   b) Au centre commercial.

   c) C'est un peu cher!

3. Est-ce que je peux vous aider?

   a) Oui, je veux acheter des chaussettes.

   b) Voilà l'argent, Madame.

   c) Je fais mes achats.

4. Où vas-tu?

   a) Au magasin.

   b) Oui, c'est tout.

   c) J'adore ce CD.

5. Le CD coûte 50,00 francs?

   a) Merci beaucoup, Mademoiselle.

   b) C'est bon marché.

   c) J'adore ce marché.

6. Quelque chose d'autre?

   a) Oui, une tomate et deux bananes, s'il vous plaît.

   b) C'est un peu cher!

   c) Ça coûte 25,00 francs.

D The conversation that follows is between a salesclerk and a customer, but the sentences are all mixed up. Rearrange them by putting them in logical order, beginning with "1" for the first sentence in the dialogue, "2" for the second sentence, etc. Number 1 is already marked for you.

_____ Voilà les baskets noirs.

_____ Noir, s'il vous plaît.

_____ Quatre cents francs.

_____ Merci. Voilà la monnaie.

_____ C'est combien?

___1___ Est-ce que je peux vous aider?

_____ Bon, j'achète les baskets noirs. Voilà l'argent, Mademoiselle.

_____ Oui, je veux des baskets.

_____ Bon, de quelle couleur?

Now, in the space below, copy all the sentences in their correct order.

1. _____

2. _____

3. _____

4. _____

5. _____

6. _____

7. _____

8. _____

9. _____

E Complete these mini-dialogues with the appropriate words.

1. Abdou: Où vas-tu?

   Jean-Paul: Au _____ commercial. Je vais acheter une chemise.

2. Vendeur: Est-ce que je peux vous aider?

   Cliente: Non, merci. Je _____ seulement.

3. Client: Ce pantalon, c'est combien?

   Vendeur: Ça _____ 200,00 francs.

4. Cliente: Le cahier, c'est cher?

   Vendeuse: Non, c'est _____ .

5. Vendeuse: Quelque chose d'autre?

   Client: _____ , merci. C'est tout.

6. Client: Où est la caissière?

   Vendeur: À la _____ .

7. Cliente: J'achète le chandail. Voilà l'argent.

   Caissière: Merci, et voilà la _____ .

F Imagine that you're at a shopping center. You and your partner play the roles of a salesclerk and a customer. Carry on a short conversation in French in which the customer makes a purchase. Limit your questions to those you have already practiced in class and be sure to respond appropriately to your partner's questions and comments. In the course of your conversation:

1) The clerk and the customer greet each other.
2) The clerk asks the customer if he or she wants some help.
3) The customer says what he or she wants to buy and asks the price of something.
4) The clerk tells the price.
5) The customer says that he or she will buy it.
6) The clerk asks if the customer wants anything else.
7) The customer says that's all and pays for the item.
8) The clerk thanks the customer and gives him or her change.

G Find your way through the store to the cash register. As you trace your route beginning at the entrance arrow, list in French each item you encounter.

_____   _____

_____   _____

_____   _____

_____

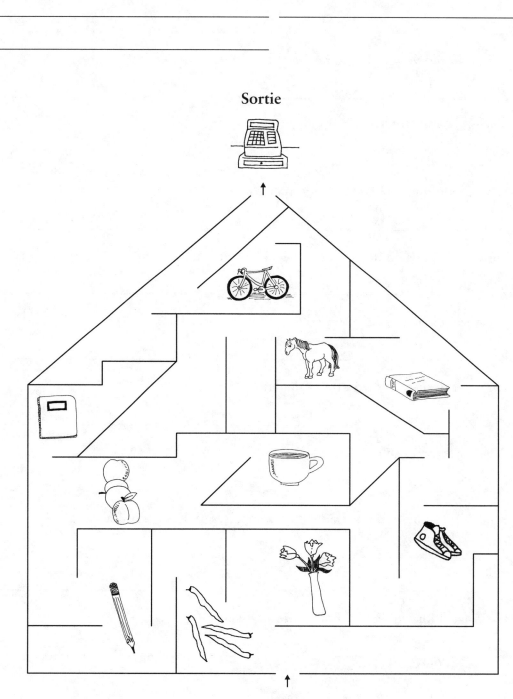

Sortie

Entrée

H You are shopping at a big French department store called BVH for the first time. You look at the store's directory to see where you need to go to buy the items on your list. Answer the following questions. You will need to know some new words: *s/s* (basement, abbreviation for *sous-sol*), *rdc* (ground floor, abbreviation for *rez-de-chaussée*), *répondeurs téléphoniques* (answering machines).

1. On what floor would you find things for the kitchen?

   _____

2. Where would you find automotive accessories?

   _____

3. Are men's and children's clothing on the same floor?

   _____

4. Where would you find sports equipment?

   _____

5. On what floor would you find musical instruments, cassettes and CDs?

   _____

6. Answering machines are on two floors. Which ones?

   _____

7. On what floor would you find calculators?

   _____

8. Where are men's shirts?

   _____

9. What determines the floor on which camping supplies are found?

   _____

   _____

10. On what floor would you find bedroom furnishings?

   _____

B H V – R I V O L I

Produit/ Etage/ Emplacement sur plan

Produit	Etage	Emplacement
ABATS-JOUR	2	c6
ABRIS DE JARDIN	s/s	d2
ADHESIFS	4	b5
ALARMES	s/s	b4
AMPOULES (déco)	2	d3
AMPOULES/FLUOS	s/s	b2
ANIMAUX (articles pour)	s/s	b1
APPLIQUES	2	d4
ARMOIRES DE RANGEMENT	6	b6
ARTS DE LA TABLE	3	b5
ASPIRATEURS	3	b2
AUTO (accessoires)	s/s	c6
BACS ET POTS	s/s	c2
BAGAGES	2	c3
BALANCES/PESE PERSONNE	3	c5
BATIMENT (matériaux)	4	c1
BIJOUTERIE	rdc	b1
BLANC	2	b4
BOIS (détail/coupe)	4	d1
BUREAU (accessoires/classement)	1	b5
CADRES/ENCADREMENT	5	c6
CAFETIERES ELECTRIQUES	3	c2
CALCULATRICES	1	d6
CAMERAS/CAMESCOPES	1	d1
CAMPING (fev./oct.)	2	a2
CAMPING (nov./janv.)	s/s	c2
CANAPES	5	c4
CARRELAGES	4	b3
CARTABLES	1	b6
CASSEROLES/COCOTTES...	3	c4
CASSETTES VIERGES	1	b1
CASSETTES ENREGISTREES	1	a3
CAVE (articles de)	s/s	a6
CHAMBRES (meubles/literie)	6	c4
CHASSE (équipement/vêtements)	2	d1
CHAUFFAGE	s/s	a1
CHEMISES HOMME	1	c3
CLIMATISEURS	3	b2
COLLANTS/BAS	rdc	d1
CONGELATEURS	3	a1
COUTELLERIE	3	c4
COUVERTURES/COUETTES...	6	a4
CRAVATES/ECHARPES	1	c3
CUISINE (articles de)	3	c3
DESSIN (accessoires pour)	1	b6
DISQUES/COMPACTS/CASSETTES	1	a3
DROGUERIE	3	d1
ECHELLES/ESCABEAUX	s/s	c1
ECLAIRAGE/BOUTIQUE HALOGENE	2	c4

B H V – R I V O L I

Produit/ Etage/ Emplacement sur plan

Produit	Etage	Emplacement
MIROITERIE D'AMEUBLEMENT	5	c1
MOQUETTE	6	d3
MOTO (accessoires/vêtements)	s/s	d6
MUSIQUE (instruments/partitions)	1	b1
NAPPES	2	a4
OPTIQUE	1	d1
OREILLERS	6	a4
ORFEVRERIE	3	b4
OUTILLAGE A MAIN	s/s	d4
OUTILLAGE DE JARDIN	s/s	c2
OUTILLAGE ELECTRIQUE	s/s	c4
PAPETERIE	1	b5
PAPIERS PEINTS	4	a4
PARAPLUIES	rdc	c5
PARFUMERIE/PRODUITS BEAUTE	rdc	a2
PASSEMENTERIE	4	b4
PECHE (équipement/vêtements)	s:s	d1
PEINTURE/BATIMENT	4	b2
PEINTURE/DESSIN	1	a6
PELLICULES/FILMS	1	d2
PHILATELIE	6	b1
PHOTO/CINEMA/CAMESCOPES	1	c1
PLAQUES DE CUISSON	3	b2
PLOMBERIE	s/s	d3
PORCELAINE	3	b5
PORTES DE PLACARDS	4	c2
PULLS DAME	rdc	c2
PULLS ENFANTS	rdc	b5
PULLS HOMME	1	c3
QUINCAILLERIE D'AMEUBLEMENT	4	c3
QUINCAILLERIE GENERALE	s/s	b4
RADIO/TELEVISION	1	b2
RASOIRS	rdc	a4
REFRIGERATEURS	3	b2
REPONDEURS TELEPHONIQUES	s/s	a3
REPONDEURS TELEPHONIQUES	1	c6
REVETEMENTS DE MUR	4	b5
REVETEMENTS DE SOL	6	d2
RIDEAUX/VOILAGES	4	d5
ROBINETTERIE	s/s	c3
SACS A DOS	2	d2
SACS A MAIN	rdc	b4
SALLE DE BAINS (accessoires)	2	b5
SECHE-LINGE	3	b1
SERRURERIE	s/s	b4
SOUDURE	s/s	d4
SOUS-VETEMENTS DAME	rdc	c2
SOUS-VETEMENTS ENFANTS	rdc	a6
SOUS-VETEMENTS HOMME	1	c3

B H V – R I V O L I

Produit/ Etage/ Emplacement sur plan

Produit	Etage	Emplacement
SPORT (vêtements/matériel)	2	c2
STORES (intérieur/extérieur)	4	c6
STYLOS	1	b5
TABLEAUX/REPRODUCTIONS	5	c6
TAPIS/TAPIS D'ORIENT	6	c1
TELEPHONES/REPONDEURS	s/s	a3
TELEPHONES/REPONDEURS	1	c6
TELEVISION/VIDEO	1	a2
TISSUS D'AMEUBLEMENT	4	c4
TOILES CIREES	6	d6
TONDEUSES A GAZON	s/s	c2
TRAVAUX PHOTO	1	d2
TRINGLES A RIDEAUX	4	d3
VAISSELLE	3	a4
VANNERIE	3	d4
VERRERIE	3	b5
VETEMENTS DAME	rdc	c3
VETEMENTS ENFANTS	rdc	b5
VETEMENTS HOMME	1	c3
VIDEO/MAGNETOSCOPES	1	a2

Unit 20

A Answer each travel question by circling the letter of the best answer.

1. Who carries a suitcase?

   a) un employé   b) un voyageur   c) un vendeur

2. What tells you arrival and departure times?

   a) un horaire   b) un billet   c) une poste

3. What permits you to travel internationally?

   a) un aller-retour   b) un billet   c) un passeport

4. Where should you keep your passport when you're traveling?

   a) dans la valise   b) au guichet   c) sur vous

5. Which expression tells you where something is?

   a) à gauche   b) à huit heures   c) attendez

6. Where can you go to buy stamps and send packages?

   a) l'Hôtel Couronne   b) la poste   c) l'aéroport

B Find the best answer in column B to each question in column A.

A		B
1. Où est la porte? _____		a) Prenez l'autobus numéro 3.
2. Et on descend où? _____		b) À neuf heures.
3. Le billet, c'est combien? _____		c) Dans la valise.
4. L'autobus part à quelle heure? _____		d) À droite.
5. Où est le passeport? _____		e) Au centre commercial.
6. Pour aller à la poste? _____		f) 150,00 francs.

C Which expression is the most appropriate answer to the question? Circle the letter of the best answer.

1. Comment vas-tu en France?

   a) En autobus.

   b) En avion.

   c) En voiture.

2. Il faut avoir le passeport?

   a) Oui, dans la valise.

   b) Oui, sur vous.

   c) Oui, à gauche.

3. Est-ce que je peux vous aider?

   a) Un aller-retour pour Paris.

   b) La poste est à gauche.

   c) Voilà le billet.

4. L'avion pour Paris part à quelle heure?

   a) Ça fait 10,00 francs.

   b) Dans quinze minutes.

   c) À la porte 79.

5. Qu'est-ce qu'il faut avoir en arrivant?

   a) Un passeport.

   b) Un billet.

   c) Un horaire.

6. Pour aller à la gare?

   a) Voilà l'horaire. L'avion part à midi.

   b) Prenez l'autobus et descendez à la poste. La gare est à droite.

   c) Attendez.... On monte à la porte 47.

D Complete each sentence with the most appropriate word in French.

1. Je voyage _____ avion.

2. Il faut avoir le passeport au _____ des passeports.

3. Le prochain train pour Paris _____ à quelle heure, Monsieur?

4. Je voudrais un aller-retour en _____ .

5. Le train arrive dans la _____ .

6. Pour _____ à l'Hôtel Couronne?

7. L'hôtel est à _____ .

8. On s'instruit en _____ .

E I. Give the French name for the means of transportation associated with each word that follows.

1. aéroport _____

2. gare _____

3. garage _____

4. océan _____

5. rue _____

II. Now write in French that you are traveling by each of these means of transportation.

1. _____

2. _____

3. _____

4. _____

5. _____

F Circle the following words, names and expressions in the letter grid. The letters may go forward or backward; they may go up, down, across or diagonally.

1. avion
2. Hôtel Couronne
3. voyages
4. autobus
5. horaire
6. moyens de transport
7. à gauche
8. aller-retour
9. voiture
10. attendez
11. poste
12. navire
13. gare
14. aéroport
15. guichet

16. à quelle heure
17. contrôle des passeports
18. valise
19. en seconde
20. rue
21. train
22. voyageuse
23. employée
24. surtout
25. d'accord
26. à droite
27. prochain
28. voudrais
29. descendez
30. Monsieur

```
            V M T G N E T I O R D A M
            O H I O D S I A R D U O V
    M S A V I O N A F A H S Y N Y S T I V S G
    J E E A T T E N D E Z E O E H C U A G A R
    R G Z I U E D L L O J T N P U A E A R U U
    D A E L R L H E L J V S S V I Q X E E Q E
    A Y D A E C A X X T D O H Q E U H R R E I
    C O N T R O L E D E S P A S S E P O R T S
    C V E Y S U B O T U A H H U D L A P P U N
    O P C I N R N R I V V E U N F L Z O R O O
    R C S O G O A V A A D H O D L E O R Y T M
    D I E S U N F D R L O C N E E H G T X R Y
    Z N D B S N S A J I E T R Y G E S I Y U V
    L A M P T E A E S S G R O L I U N N S S E
    P T O B R S P G N E E L C H O R A I R E T
    Q R A L A H D E Q T P B E S U E G A Y O V
    T E H C I U G C O M J D B Z M F Z I A R D
            N C I U E P R O C H A I N
            T E R I V A N C E S H U L
```

G Imagine that you're in a French train station. You and your partner play the roles of a clerk at the ticket counter and a traveler. Carry on a short conversation in French in which the traveler buys a train ticket. Limit your questions to those you have already practiced in class and be sure to respond appropriately to your partner's questions and comments. In the course of your conversation:

1) The clerk and the traveler greet each other.
2) The traveler tells the clerk what city he or she is going to and asks at what time the next train for that city is leaving.
3) The clerk tells the traveler the time.
4) The traveler tells the clerk that he or she wants a round-trip ticket in second class and asks the price.
5) The clerk tells the traveler the price.
6) The traveler pays for the ticket.
7) The clerk thanks the traveler and gives him or her change.

H You are spending your vacation traveling in France trying to see as much as you can. You decide to take the train from Paris to Quimper. Study the train schedules for 19 of the many trains that serve this region and answer the questions that follow. You will need to know some new words: *circule* (runs), *tous les jours* (every day), *sauf* (except), *fêtes* (holidays).

Numéro de train		89175	87775	89231/0	87587	3617	8639	8843	89179	8947	6934/5	87579	3861	87765/4	8647	87595	87523	3741	8755	8861
Notes à consulter		1	2	3	4	5	6	7	8	9	10	11	12		13		2	9	14	15
							TGV	TGV	TGV						TGV				TGV	TGV
Paris-Montparnasse 1-2	D					15.02	15.20	15.40	16.15			16.19		16.20			16.43	17.20	17.50
Massy	D						I	I	I			I		I			I	I	I
Le Mans	D						16.57	I	I			18.20		17.15			18.30	I	18.46
Laval	D						17.43	I	I			I		17.57		18.03	19.14	I	I
Rennes	D	16.48			16.51	18.28	17.24	I	17.36	I		17.40	I	18.22	18.33	18.43	18.58	20.25	19.27	I
Nantes	D	I		17.30	I			17.46	I	18.18	18.23	I	19.57	I		I		I	I	20.01
Redon	A	17.24	17.32	18.12	17.46				18.16	19.01	19.14	18.48		19.04		19.46		21.03	I	
Questembert	A	I	17.52						18.34	I	I							21.20	I	
Vannes	A	17.51	18.08						18.49	19.27	19.41							21.35	20.24	
Auray	A	18.05	18.24						19.03	19.41	19.54							21.49	I	
Hennebont	A	18.21	18.50						I	I	20.11							22.06	I	
Lorient	A	18.29	18.57						19.23	20.00	20.18							22.14	20.50	
Quimperlé	A	18.47							19.37		20.32							22.28	I	
Rosporden	A	19.06							19.54		20.48							22.45	I	
Quimper	A	19.20							20.08		21.02							22.59	21.25	

Pour compléter votre information veuillez consulter les fiches horaires régionales.

1. If you want to go from Paris to Quimper as fast as possible, you take the high-speed train called the TGV. What is the number of the only TGV that goes directly from Paris to Quimper?

_____

2. If you take this TGV, at what time do you leave Paris and at what time do you arrive in Quimper?

_____

Notes

1. Circule : jusqu'au 2 juil : les ven;les 3, 10, 17 et 24 sept- 🛒 .
2. 🚲 .
3. Circule : tous les jours sauf les sam- 🚲 .
4. Circule : jusqu'au 2 juil et à partir du 6 sept : tous les jours sauf les sam, dim et fêtes- 2ᵉ CL- 🚲 .
5. Circule : les ven- 🛒 - ♿ .
6. 🍷 - ♿ .
7. Circule : jusqu'au 4 juil : tous les jours sauf les sam et sauf le 30 mai;Circule du 9 juil au 29 août : les ven, dim et fêtes;à partir du 30 août : tous les jours sauf les sam- 🍷 - ♿ .
8. 🛒 .
9. Circule : les ven- 🍷 - ♿ .
10. 🛒 assuré certains jours- 🍷 - ♿ .
11. Circule : tous les jours sauf les sam, dim et fêtes.
12. Circule : les ven- 🍷 assuré certains jours- ♿ .
13. Circule : tous les jours sauf les sam et sauf le 30 mai- 🍷 - ♿ .
14. Circule : tous les jours sauf les sam, dim et fêtes- 🍷 - ♿ .
15. Circule : tous les jours sauf les ven- 🍷 - ♿ .
16. Circule : les ven- 🚲 .
17. Circule : les dim et fêtes.
18. Circule : les lun, mar, mer, jeu sauf les 31 mai et 14 juil- 📷 1ʳᵉ CL assuré certains jours- 🍷 - ♿ .
19. Circule : les ven- 🛒 assuré certains jours- 🍷 - ♿ .
20. Circule : les lun, mar, mer, jeu sauf les 31 mai et 14 juil- 🚲 .
21. Circule : les sam et le 30 mai.
22. Circule : du 4 juil au 29 août : les dim.
23. 📷 1ʳᵉ CL assuré certains jours- 🍷 - ♿ .

Symboles

A	Arrivée		🛏	Couchettes		♿	Facilités handicapés
D	Départ		🛏	Voiture-lits			
			✕	Voiture-restaurant			
TGV	Résa TGV : réservation obligatoire		⊗	Grill-express		🚲	Vélo
			📷	Restauration à la place			
			🍷	Bar			
⇄	Cabine 8		🛒	Vente ambulante			

3. On which days of the week doesn't this train run?

   _____

4. Does this train have facilities for handicapped travelers?

   _____

5. How many stops does this train make before it arrives in Quimper?

   _____

6. What is the number of the only non-TGV train that goes directly from Paris to Quimper?

   _____

7. How long does this train trip take?

   _____

8. What is the only day of the week that this train runs?

   _____

9. How many stops does this train make before it arrives in Rennes?

   _____

10. If you want to travel by TGV between Paris and Rennes, how many different trains can you take? What are their numbers?

   _____